"*Emotional Weight* is a fresh look at the causes of weight problems and their solutions, shedding new insight on an age-old problem."

— Bettie B. Youngs, Ph.D.
Author of *Helping Your Teenager Deal with Stress*

"*An absolute must* ... I recommend this book to everyone who wants to get in touch with their true emotions and establish a healthy way of eating that keeps you strong."

— Debra E. Beaubrie, R.N., M.S.N.

EMOTIONAL WEIGHT

Colleen A. Sundermeyer, Ph.D.

New Outlook
6373 Riverside Boulevard
Sacramento, California
Box 114   95831

Printed in the United States of America

To my darling husband Mark,
who has helped me experience
the emotion of true love.

Table of Contents

Order Form for Cassette Tapes inside back cover

Preface

This book is a message of hope for those who want to be healthy, happy, thin, and in control of eating. It will help you feel confident in helping yourself better understand your emotions and identify what you want out of life and how to obtain it. You will learn new ways to challenge your eating problems successfully by looking at mind and body. Good health depends on maintaining a balance of both psychological and nutritional levels.

The concepts and information in *Emotional Weight* are the result of not only my education in nutrition and psychology, but of more than 6000 hours of counseling people with eating problems such as obesity, compulsive overeating, anorexia and bulimia. This book discusses the psychological and nutritional reasons for eating problems and their solutions.

There is no typical anorexic or bulimic person. He or she can be your next-door neighbor who just wants to lose a few pounds, or the 60-year-old man or woman who has dieted all their life. Eating problems are not exclusively a young person's problem. Anyone can have an eating problem. An eating problem can occur during times of change when there is a lot of stress, anxious feelings, self-doubt, and uncertainty about the future. All of these feelings can cause people to turn to or away from food for comfort and control. During these stressful times people may isolate themselves, feeling they must deal with these feelings alone, and the refrigerator is always there for comfort.

The reason 79% of the people who have eating problems are between the ages of 13 and 22 is that this is a time of great change, especially for the teenager who is experiencing physical, social, and emotional changes. Turning to or away from food becomes a coping mechanism and a way to express emotional pain associated with these changes. These people need to learn a healthy way to cope with the stress of trying to reach their goals, and the frustration of never having enough time in a day.

Eating problems fall into a wide range of ages (11-60), races, and socioeconomic groups for both men and women. I believe these problems should therefore be treated as individual cases with unique symptoms, causes, and needs. I try to reach people before their eating problem presents a medical danger requiring hospitalization. I do, however, provide support for people who need hospitalization. I feel the best treatment is a supportive and caring approach, while also being direct and authoritative, allowing room to explore what works best for each person.

Obesity, anorexia, and bulimia are not new occurrences. Obesity, however, is associated with social disapproval, which makes this problem more visible than anorexia and bulimia. Even though anorexics may appear severely underweight, being thin is still socially more acceptable and is seen as attractive for women. The reverse can hold true for men in our society: thin men are seen as "skinny," and overweight men can be viewed as "stocky." Don't get me wrong—men can have eating problems, too, despite what is viewed as a more positive label. I work with a lot of men with eating problems, and they share a great many similarities with women!

Bulimia is a hidden problem. While binging and purging daily, the bulimic can be of normal weight. The anorexic shares similar traits with the bulimic, sometimes engaging in bouts of overeating (binging) and vomiting (purging) when food restriction becomes less acceptable to them. Once this happens, this person is no longer just anorexic, but a bulimic/anorexic. Laxatives, diuretics, diet pills, and enemas are used by the bulimic or anorexic to continue in this vicious cycle.

Did you know that not all anorexics are drastically underweight? Some can be of normal body weight or even overweight, but restrict their food intake to 500 calories or less a day. Think about it! Many people who are dieting fall into this calorie range. Diets encourage the restriction of food, telling us that the more we deprive ourselves the better we are supposed to feel. What starts out to be a positive healthy change to better fulfill one's needs ends up being physical and emotional self-deprivation.

Even though it would appear that food is to blame for these eating problems, it is not. Severe food restriction, overeating, binging, purging, overexercising, or preoccupation with body weight are not the causes of these problems. These are merely the symptoms! Such activities are the best way these individuals know how to cope with life's difficulties and with emotions that are too frightening to face! *Emotional Weight* will provide people with a healthier way of coping, helping them to learn self-fulfilling behaviors, not self-depriving behaviors. This book will help people realize that physical weight is not the cause of the problem, but rather the emotional problems are the cause of the physical weight problem.

Above all, these people are not alone! Even people with long-term eating problems *can* and *do recover!* Recovery means not just losing fat, or for the anorexic, eating again, or for the bulimic, stopping binging and purging. Recovery means developing a *positive self-image* and *peace of mind!*

Acknowledgments

I am truly grateful to the many people who shared their experiences and insights in order to make this book a reality. Special love and thanks are given to: Andrea Amptman, Debbie Beaudrie, Robert Merino, Loren Anderson, Philip Schneider, Steve Wright, Herb Miessner, and Steven Huczek for their love and support. I would also like to thank Dr. Simeon Wade, Dr. Herbert W. Haberland, Dr. Frank Sutter, Gerald Shannon, and Phyllis Young for their kindness, strength, and encouragement.

I wish to acknowledge my editor and typesetter, Jon Lewis, for his faith in this project, and for the many hours he spent working late into the night. (Jon, see page 124!)

Introduction

Is thinner happier? It seems most Americans think so. We spend about ten million dollars each year to be thin. The belief that thinner is happier has a lot of approval in our culture. The power of social approval comes from the way we view it.

If we perceive or label social approval as rewarding and believe that being thin leads to social approval, the credo that "thinner is happier" will be accepted. We receive continuous reinforcement of this notion as we are bombarded with advertisements from TV, magazines, and billboards promoting the thin ideal. Be the *perfect weight* and have the *perfect life!*

This book emphasizes the concept that *controlling eating means controlling the mind.* Therefore, the way we perceive ourselves and events in our lives determines how we will react. We can give ourselves and certain events a great deal of power just by the way we label them, positively or negatively. In order for us to use our full potential and achieve a permanent, healthy body weight, we must look at both *mind* and *body,* since it is our thoughts that first create the label. Even though we tend to give more attention to the food we feed our bodies, equal attention must be given to the thoughts we feed our minds. Just as we take the time to feed our bodies nutritious food for good physical health, so must we feed our minds positive thoughts for good mental health. The first step to permanent weight control must be to begin thinking more positively. It is the negative thoughts and attitudes that keep people holding onto their eating problems.

Thinking positively is cost-free and doesn't require any more energy than thinking negatively. So stop thinking you *have* to achieve ideal body weight, and instead think that you *want* to. No one likes to *have* to do anything. We all have choices in life, all of which we are responsible for. In other words, we choose what we think. No one can make you eat that piece of chocolate cream pie. You choose to eat it. Then you again choose how you want to label your actions. Are you going to label eating the piece of pie as a reflection of being weak, hopeless, having no willpower, and as the end of your weight control plan? Instead, label eating the piece of pie as OK, it was a choice, *not* a major setback.

Keep in mind that most of us need to make mistakes and reset our goals, trying several new directions before finding what works best for us. Don't get hung up on small mistakes. Rather, take them in stride. Mistakes are really opportunities in disguise and are part of our learning process, making us more self-aware. Don't forget, you are only human. Allow yourself room to make mistakes. Chapter Two discusses this concept. No one can be a *perfect* person, and achieving that *perfect* weight doesn't mean the solution to your problems. Negative feelings, low self-esteem, self-doubt, anger, hate, fear, happiness, and disappointment are not stored in your fat tissue. Losing fat doesn't mean you lose these feelings or your identity. You're still going to be you. Continuing to believe that your physical weight is the cause of your problems, and not recognizing that your problems are the cause of your eating problem, only delays getting to the root of the problem. Eating problems are merely the *symptoms,* not the cause!

As human beings, we tend to look toward the simpler, more pleasurable solution when trying to overcome a problem. Eating is a much more pleasurable way to deal with a problem than facing our emotions or disappointments in life. I'm sure you would agree! We are much more certain we can control what goes in and out of our mouths.

Another important concept is to give yourself credit for your accomplishments, no matter how small you think they are. Self-approval is a powerful motivational tool. Unfortunately, numerous diets give little attention to self-approval, but only to disapproval. Diets give support to the perfectionist self-critical person, especially in cases of eating problems. Diets leave no room for mistakes. Diet programs require the diet be followed exactly if the person wishes to succeed. If not, they have failed. As you can imagine, failure isn't taken lightly by the overly perfectionist person and usually ends in some type of *self-punishment* like overeating, stepping on the scale and then going on another diet. Often, an association develops as diets and food become synonymous with punishment, guilt, and self-deprivation, often leading to more severe, life-threatening behavior. Dieting has kept people overweight and self-critical, creating a severe loss of self-esteem. Eating is seen as a sign of *vulnerability.* The "dieter" is told that the less you eat the better you are supposed to feel, when in reality the less you eat the worse you feel!

Lastly, people who have lost weight through dieting only to quickly gain it back learn how to *avoid* food, not *control* food. I believe that the more food is avoided the more people learn not to trust themselves. When they eat the "forbidden" foods, it only reinforces the distrust they already have in themselves. Taking things to extremes and behaving rigidly are the first signs that you do not trust yourself. When you label foods forbidden or bad, and then eat them, it usually triggers feelings of guilt and then some form of self-punishment. Labeling food "bad" gives it *power!* It is the feeling of guilt that triggers binging, along with many other self-punishing behaviors. Never forget: punishment only serves to repress immediate actions, and is not useful for making long-term, permanent changes.

The chronic dieter and drug addict share a similarity. Both began with what they believed to be a harmless attempt at improving their lives. Without even realizing it, both move toward a more desperate attempt to improve self-esteem and control their lives. The chronic dieter begins to binge and purge, and the drug addict moves to a harder, longer-lasting drug. Both people were just trying to gain a little self-esteem and control, which resulted in a fearful *overcontrol,* using dangerous and even life-threatening means. The fear of not being in charge of one's life can be a petrifying feeling. Most diet programs set the pace, telling the dieter how much weight should be lost within a designated time, such as 4 to 10 pounds in one week. Every person is different, and must learn to set their own pace and goals, not what someone else decides. People must listen to their bodies.

I believe effective counseling involves helping people make better choices, not making choices for them. Focusing also on the *process*, not just the *end goal.* When choices are made for people and then they fail, they become even more self-critical, making such statements as, "What's wrong with me? I can't even control my weight." They feel that they have tried and *failed* to live up to the expectations of someone else and then they simply quit trying, feeling hopeless and above all *tired!*

Everyone's weight control goals should be tailor-made to fit their own needs—both nutritional and psychological. We must learn that the responsibility for our weight control goals lies within ourselves, *not* the diet per se. How many times have you heard, "Oh, that diet really worked"? This person failed to recognize that he or she was the one that worked, not the diet. *People work, not diets!*

Of equal importance is the idea that we tend to be an instant society, wanting things right away. Frequently in life we are used to immediate results. If we want a quick meal there are fast food restaurants; if we need gas quickly there are self-serve stations; and if we want quick weight loss, there are pills, magic creams and drinks, or another new diet on the market, promising quick, easy, instant results. Remember, you're not making oatmeal, you're changing your life, and progress is made step by step. Progress requires time for you to succeed and stick with your health goals. As Thomas Edison said, "Our greatest human weakness lies in giving up too soon."

This book looks past appearance and vanity to help people see more than just what is in the mirror or on the scale. Achieving ideal body weight means a lot more than just *losing fat!* It must incorporate both *mind* and *body*. *Emotional Weight* looks at creating positive attitudes by changing your beliefs and opinions through new learning experiences, taking what you learn and applying it to real life experiences. Although I do believe your attitude does initially create the behavior, it must periodically be reinforced, usually through positive experiences. If not, positive behavior quickly ends. If you are trying to achieve weight control and you do not experience positive reinforcement quickly enough, you may want to quit.

You want it *now!* Learning to be patient is the key, and labeling ourselves and events positively provides the time needed to succeed. Without patience, people will always fall short of their goals, and without action we go nowhere. We must get off our fannies and *go for it!*

Another important concept in this book is that *all* emotions are good. Even guilt, fear, anger, and disappointment are positive and good emotions. When emotions are used in a positive way, they can provide people with a better sense of who they are and where they want to go in life. Yes, emotions can do all that, if you listen to them. Emotions are all a natural part of you and emotions can't be *stopped* any more than an involuntary response like blinking your eyes. However, each of us can control what we do *about them*. We can accept and trust our emotions, or we can deny or repress them. It is when we repress them that they are no longer working in a positive way. This is when we begin to form *emotional weight*. By fighting our true emotions, the more we turn to or away from food for comfort and control. Food is then functioning as a temporary escape or satisfaction, further delaying getting to the root of the problem. *Emotions were meant to be expressed.* If they are not expressed, fear, happiness, love, doubt, and anger can all be displaced onto food. Eating or not eating temporarily reduces the anxiety, but the problem is still there!

Sometimes eating problems become a necessary part of a person's life, and the fear of losing the dependency on food is much stronger than the eating problem itself. Anorexics and bulimics find their eating problem makes them unique, and they are given a lot of attention, care, and love because of their problem. Therefore, recovery means they may not continue to receive these affections. Eating problems can become a way of communicating without having to take a verbal risk, and they may live in fear of losing this once they are seen as having recovered. They can't say, "I'm hurting." Instead, emotions are expressed by physically damaging their bodies, making their hurt visible.

These people are carrying *emotional weight*, which is reflected in their distorted body image. For them the mirror image will never be good enough, thin enough, or beautiful enough, until they lose their emotional weight. Emotional weight can't be seen in the mirror or on the scale, but it is there, reflected in the 95% of the people who regain their physical weight. When emotional weight is left untreated, physical weight will always return, and the thin person will never feel thin enough. The heaviness lies in their minds in the form of emotional weight, as they develop physical intimacy with food, instead of emotional intimacy with themselves.

By repressing our true emotions, we may find ourselves eating in negative mood states, feeling out of control of our actions. Eating then becomes more of a mechanical experience. This is why a person can eat and eat and never feel satisfied, because the hunger is not a *physical* hunger but an *emotional* hunger. Once you learn to practice the three A's—*awareness, admittance,* and *acceptance* of your emotions—realizing it is okay to feel anger, hurt, fear, disappointment, and even happiness, you'll no longer turn to or away from food for comfort and control. Express the feelings; lose the physical and emotional weight.

Emotional weight can be seen in some anorexics and bulimics. These people are sometimes dangerously thin but still feel they are overweight. They are eating food during negative mood states, adding weight not in body but in *mind.* I have observed hundreds of people who eat in negative mood states, causing them to feel as though they have overeaten and to feel extremely heavy, even though they have eaten very little. This feeling of heaviness lies in the mind in the form of *emotional weight.* People who are chronic dieters, anorexic, or bulimic feel a sense of power and gratification from their problem. These people are not weak. However, their energy does need to be redirected in a healthy, positive way, while providing them with the same feeling of power and gratification they have been receiving from their eating problem. They need help and direction, and to learn that it is okay to reach out and need people. Receiving help doesn't mean you are *helpless.*

This book takes a good long look at *nutrition* and getting back to the basics of *healthy* eating—not ritual eating, where you can eat only fruit in the morning and carbohydrates in the afternoon. This is just the kind of behavior and preoccupation with food that I see in cases of anorexia and bulimia. Diets encourage people to develop eating problems with this kind of eating style! In this book, I discuss the American diet and how it has changed. I discuss how fat is burned, and how the body recognizes fat as *survival.* Eating smaller, more frequent meals is demonstrated in this book as an important way to stay healthy and control *physical* weight.

The vitamin and mineral section discusses which supplements are needed to keep a strong, healthy body, especially when trying to lose fat, without threatening your *set point.* For years I have been using the nutritional techniques I suggest in my book with great success. I explain what carbohydrates, proteins, and fats are, and how they function in the body to keep your health. I teach people to *stop* viewing food in terms of *destructive calories.* Suggestions on how to improve digestion and intestinal flora, as well as how laxatives work—or I should say *don't* work—at reducing calorie absorption. More suggestions are given on what foods and supplements can be used safely to reduce stress, get rid of headaches, lower cholesterol, and eliminate fatigue and depression, and several tips are provided on nutritional labeling, meats, dairy products, and much more. I will discuss exercise and how it effects your mind and body, as well as what foods are needed more when exercising in order to stay strong and build the muscle to burn fat.

Emotional Weight will provide you with a healthier way of coping, helping you learn *self-fulfilling* behaviors, not self-depriving behaviors.

EMOTIONAL
WEIGHT

PART I

LOOKING AT MIND

Human potential —

Beyond comprehension

But never beyond us

— Doug Poppenger

Feed Your Mind the Right Thoughts

Often, in talking about weight control, we talk only about the food we feed our bodies. We give little attention to the thoughts we feed our minds. We have become a diet-conscious, calorie-counting society. Why? Because we realize that the body does reflect the food it is fed. Our strength, stamina, resistance to disease, body size, and mental health are all related to what we feed our bodies. By the same token, the mind reflects the thoughts it is fed. Clearly, then, equal attention must be given to developing a healthy mind and body.

Your thoughts are very powerful. They play a large role in the outcome of whatever it is you want to achieve. You develop a subjective probability or personal estimate of the likelihood that your effort, such as eating well or exercising, will lead to your desired outcome. Have you ever said, "I can't even walk by a bakery without gaining ten pounds," or "I just can't lose weight and keep it off"? All the thoughts you think produce changes in your feelings, leading to actions and finally to reactions in yourself and others. You need to become more aware that the negative thoughts you feed your mind are just as self-destructive as eating the wrong kinds of foods.

If you eat foods high in fat, sugars, and salt, you usually show visible signs: indigestion, gas, diarrhea, high blood pressure, diabetes, weight gain, etc. These signals help you, telling you that eating like this is not good for you. The negative thoughts you continue to feed your mind have much more subtle signals and are not always as observable. Of course, there is still a consequence to your negative thinking. You may begin to have feelings of hopelessness or a sort of down-in-the-dumps feeling, not quite knowing why you feel unhappy. Negative thinking doesn't make you feel good about life, and life is what you make of it. Life is seen by the positive thinker as challenging and full of hope. In contrast, the negative thinker looks at life as boring, nothing but a struggle.

POSITIVE THINKING

Learning to think positively requires organization, time, and discipline, as well as cognitive restructuring. In other words, you need to clean up your thoughts— just as you clean your house once a week. A house seems to collect a lot of items, some of which will be useful, others that only cause more confusion.

So you clean it up, getting rid of the useless items, while saving the more important ones. Similar clutter occurs in your mind. You collect years of good and bad experiences, which can cause either negative or positive feelings about yourself. Get rid of the negative thoughts that cause more confusion, only fostering self-defeating, pessimistic attitudes and low self-esteem. Decide, "This is my life and I'm going to *clean it up!*"

One possible way to achieve a positive attitude is to think of your mind as if it were a computer. A computer must be programmed with the correct information in order for it to work; so, too, must your mind be programmed with the correct thoughts. You need to develop attitude goals as well as weight control goals, bringing the mind and body together. Perhaps the reason why ninety-five percent of the people who lose physical weight gain it back within one year is that they haven't made mind *and* body changes. Something was missing. The mental changes never occurred with the physical changes. Physical weight was lost, but emotional weight remained. If emotional weight is left untreated, sooner or later turning to or away from food for comfort and control recurs. This can be seen in a person who loses physical weight, yet still feels heavy. This person may be a size ten in clothes but still shops for a size fourteen. Why? The heaviness may lie more in the mind of the individual, in the form of "emotional weight," than in the body. In such instances a person may be thin but still not happy, healthy, and in control of eating. You must feel good about yourself inside to feel good about what you see on the outside. The mirror image will never seem thin enough, good enough, or beautiful enough until you feel good about yourself inside. The next time you look in the mirror, really look—deep into your eyes. There is a lot of beauty inside all of us.

You can't continue to view the body and mind separately when trying to achieve weight control, because emotional weight is in your mind and physical weight is in your body. Look at yourself as a whole person— not just as *hips and thighs*. Start by cleaning up your thinking process. You're eating healthier, better quality foods and thinking healthier, better quality thoughts. Take a piece of paper once a week and write down some of your negative, self-defeating thoughts about yourself: fears, anger, disappointments and hostile thoughts—"I don't care" attitudes. Then on another piece of paper, write down some positive thoughts and actions that will help you rid yourself of overwhelming negativity. Start saying *"I do care."* When you write your positive

thoughts down and start thinking about them, they are
no longer just thoughts, but are now more alive, and
represent goals. We all know how important water is,
and without it we would die. Keeping a positive attitude is just as important to the mind as water is to the
body. If we don't keep a positive attitude, our goals
simply die.

Take the piece of paper with the negative thoughts
and crumple it up and throw it away. Now, write down
five or ten positive things you like about yourself. Don't
hold back if you think of more! Focus each day on your
positive qualities, and *stop* punishing yourself with negative thoughts and actions over something you did last
week, yesterday, or even two hours ago. It is over, so
go on and focus on the present. Take your time and really think about and identify with what you are writing
down. Don't just write words—really *feel* them! It is
only natural that you could write about fifteen pages on
what you believe are your negative qualities and barely
get out a word about your good qualities. This indicates that you still need to get to know yourself. It is
time you meet yourself, and this exercise helps you do
just that! The first step would be to start *now*—not
tomorrow or Monday, or even "someday,"—but NOW!
Immediately write down on a piece of paper, "I can
and will achieve a healthy, permanent body weight; I
am healthy, happy, and in control of eating." Each
time you want to quit, pull out your goals and review
them. Do this a couple of times a day, especially when
you have thoughts of giving up! Positive thinking is a
much healthier idea than binging and purging, or using diet pills or laxatives which have many dangerous
side effects psychologically and physically. Each time
you feed your mind good thoughts and your body good
food, it is a wonderful spiritual message. It says. "I
care about myself and good things are going to happen! I *deserve* good things! There are also side effects

that result from positive thinking: *a positive self-image and peace of mind!*

Positive thinking is easy when everything is going well for you, but very difficult when things are somewhat chaotic. This is when you need to apply it most of all! Positive thinking doesn't always provide you with instant results, just like taking a vitamin and mineral supplement doesn't always provide instant health. Yet it is still working for you. Your mind is powerful—*use it!* Every thought you think will eventually produce either positive or negative changes in your life. For most of us, learning to ride a bike meant we had to *get back on* many times, trying new ways to sit on or balance your bike. Overcoming an eating problem also requires you keep trying to discover how to find that *healthy balance* in life, and positive thinking allows you to find out what works best for you. It's when you are the most tired and want to say, "I just don't care," that you are *almost up the hill.*

Nonverbal thoughts also contribute significantly to your behaviors and emotions, and can be used to change undesirable behavior. You can't just sit around and think positively in hopes that fat will melt from your thighs, or that you can overcome anorexia or bulimia by just "thinking yourself better." You can't just think yourself into a size eight bikini; you don't build muscles just by thinking about them. Most change requires action. Start by saying, "I'm important," and then make some important changes in your behavior, taking it a step at a time. If you try too much too soon, you're going to trip and feel discouraged. The positive thoughts initiate the positive actions which cause the positive reactions. Therefore, overcoming an eating problem requires cognitive (mind) and behavioral (action) components. What we have just discussed might seem rather basic, but it is the basics in life that work! The more technical or complicated ideas are sometimes too difficult to understand and apply. Getting back to

the basics means using your own potential. To discover
your potential you must think positively.

Negative thinking just fills you with fear and doubt,
moving you farther from discovering your potential for
recovery.

SUSAN

Susan, a thirty-five-year-old woman and mother of
two, learned to get back to the basics. Susan was working part-time in an office. She felt very insecure due
to her demanding boss, coupled with her desire to lose
about 65 pounds that she had been struggling with for
five years. When she walked into my office she expressed
how disappointed she was in herself; she claimed always
to be angry and short with people. One of the goals
I suggested for Susan was to look in the mirror each
morning and really look into her eyes, repeating the
words, "I'm important!" Well, Susan thought I had a
few screws loose to request such a task, yet she continued to do it. This was an especially difficult task for her
because looking in the mirror was not something she enjoyed. After one month she began to take notice of not
only the way she looked, but the way she thought. Susan noticed that she had really changed when her angry
boss called her incompetent. She immediately thought,
"No, I'm not ... I'm important!" This was a new attitude that Susan never thought she would have about
herself.

Susan hadn't lost physical weight, yet she was feeling lighter and good about herself. Looking in the mirror into her eyes was not so difficult anymore. Susan
glowed with pride when she said, "Before I would have
been so devastated with what my boss said that I would
have quit my job and put myself in a financial bind,
making the situation even worse." This was a big step
for Susan, as she began to recognize how low self-esteem

(emotional weight) was the cause of her physical weight, not the other way around. Finally, Susan put an end to her quick weight loss ideas and started getting to the root of the problem. For Susan, it was much easier to blame her physical weight than to deal with the real cause. And the more she continued to think positively, the more she gained confidence in expressing her feelings. Experiencing a sense of control in her life, no longer did she turn to or away from food for comfort and control. Susan lost 55 pounds of emotional weight and 55 pounds of physical weight (fat). At our last session Susan grinned as she told me that she no longer needed her regular scale, and her *emotional* scale now read *"peace of mind!"*

Positive thinking is a powerful tool. Positive thinking causes positive behavior, which then must be periodically reinforced, usually through a feeling of accomplishment which comes by acknowledging both your smallest and biggest successes. Give yourself credit! If reinforcement of this kind does not occur, your behavior usually ends—you simply stop trying. This is one reason why many people can successfully control their physical weight for only one week and then they quit. These necessary reinforcers could also be called *motivators*. You must develop internal as well as external motivators so you can keep moving forward. Your thoughts are powerful, and even though controlling your physical weight means controlling what you eat, it really means controlling your *mind!* Think about it. We all have heard about the power of suggestion, or the placebo effect. These effects are real, but we can't scientifically explain why. Start bringing positive suggestions into your mind so you lose emotional weight and, if necessary, permanently lose physical weight. Your actions are not controlled by some unknown extraterrestrial force. They are within your control.

JESSE

Jesse didn't believe she was in control of her emotions or her life. She believed she was a victim of circumstances. Her belief in this idea was strong—so strong that she was creating her own personal disasters. I wanted to help Jesse use that strong negative belief and turn it into a strong positive belief.

This meant learning to listen to herself and then trust what she was hearing. Let me tell you a little more about Jesse.

At age 31, Jesse had developed a destructive pattern of self-punishment. When Jesse ate what she considered "forbidden" foods like chocolate chip cookies or double fudge ripple ice cream, she immediately felt a need to punish herself by severely restricting food and frantically exercising. Little did Jesse know she was actually creating negative feelings toward exercise and food. These were now activities used to punish herself.

As we counseled, Jesse realized that punishing herself was a way to reduce her guilt, and that guilt wasn't something to repress by self-punishment, but rather a natural emotion she should allow to surface and be expressed.

I explained to Jesse that self-punishment usually represses immediate behavior (i.e., it might prevent her from eating a bag of cookies), but is not effective in making long-term changes and only serves to lower self-esteem. These concepts were difficult for Jesse because expressing her emotions was frightening. She would therefore rationalize food to be the source of her problem; she found that prospect less frightening to talk about. In our first few sessions she would steer our conversation toward food and always away from the real problem—*self-expression*. I kept moving Jesse toward more expression of her emotions.

Jesse felt extremely vulnerable when expressing her emotions; she feared not being accepted by others. I constantly reinforced the idea that self-expression is essential to forming a stable identity, and to better understanding just who she was. Slowly, I helped Jesse identify with her emotions as she accepted that love, trust, guilt, anger, and vulnerability were emotions that she was repressing by focusing on food as the problem. Once Jesse became comfortable with expressing her feelings to me, she gradually opened up and began expressing herself to her family and friends.

You might be wondering exactly how much weight Jesse lost. Actually, she was not overfat. Jesses's heaviness was in her mind, not her body, in the form of *emotional weight*.

IT'S YOUR CHOICE

On many occasions people have asked me whether I believe fat cells are determined genetically or influenced by early nutrition. Since I'm educated in both psychology and nutrition, the only way to answer is to state that each of us is a product of many things. You are a product of what you eat, and a product of your environment. It is, therefore, presently impossible to absolutely separate genetic factors from other factors. Nevertheless, *there is something you can do!* You have freedom of choice. Freedom comes with responsibility. This concept has made a wonderful difference in a great number of people's lives. For example, several of my clients have questioned why it is that during our counseling I just don't immediately tell them what they have to do. I believe that people have to have freedom of choice. If I were to tell one of my clients, "Mary, you have to stop eating Oreo cookies with the creamy white center," what do you think Mary is going to eat when she is upset—a carrot stick or an Oreo cookie with the creamy white center? Yes, you're right—an Oreo cookie, and probably more than just one. No one likes to *have to do* anything. You like to choose for yourself. You can make good choices for yourself if just given the chance.

MACK

Mack first came to see me because he wanted to lose weight. He was a competitive runner and felt that losing a few pounds would help his performance. Mack had recently had a complete physical and was told by his doctor that he might have anorexic tendencies because he was quite a bit underweight already, but still felt that he needed to lose more. When Mack entered the office, he expressed his disappointment that I was a woman, and assumed that I would know nothing about competitive running. As I talked with him, I could tell that he was obsessed with losing physical weight. He did most of the talking during our session, and when I tried to talk to him he quickly interrupted. Mack kept saying that he didn't really need my help. Through this behavior I could see that Mack had a strong need to be in charge all the time, and had a hard time letting down his defenses. When I asked him why he came to see me if he really didn't need help, he replied, "My neurotic doctor told me I was anorexic, but I know anorexia happens only to women."

I asked him what he had been eating, and how many calories he was consuming. He told me that he had been on a "liquid diet" and had only been drinking fruit juices. I asked him if he was experiencing muscle fatigue, and whether his endurance during running had diminished. This was the first time Mack looked directly at me as I gained his interest. Mack had the attitude that everyone was stupid and challenged me until he realized I knew what I was talking about. I then gave Mack a tape of a lecture I had done on sports nutrition and told him if he felt he learned anything from it after listening to it, he should come back to see me. At this point, I was giving Mack the chance to make his own choice by allowing him the control he so desperately craved.

When Mack returned a week later, he told me he really liked the tape, but had a list of questions. He needed to challenge me just once more.

I gave a great deal of thought on how best to handle Mack, who had a hard time accepting help. I decided initially to focus on improving his endurance and strength in running rather than focusing on weight gain, allowing him gradually to make that choice of his own free will. I knew if I told Mack that he had to gain physical weight, he would have stubbornly rebelled by losing more weight to show that me he was in charge.

Even though Mack showed no physical gain for the first month, he wasn't losing weight. This was progress! Once Mack began to trust and respect me, he became more open to my suggestions, as I watched him slowly gain weight.

Mack never weighed himself, and began listening to his own body needs. He began to trust himself, feeling *he* was in charge, not the scale. When he did tell me that he was gaining weight, I responded with, "Good! Are you feeling stronger? Is your running time improving?" I always reinforced the importance of nutritional nourishment in order to achieve peak performance. Within six months Mack had achieved a healthy body weight and was no longer restricting food. He gained more confidence in himself so that he didn't always need to be in charge. I heard from Mack several months later. He told me he was allowing more people to share his life by allowing himself to need others. He began to realize that the more he accepted needing others, the more confident he became. Mack said he no longer felt ashamed and alone with his eating problem, and had stopped trying to pretend he was fine.

Too many quick weight control organizations offer no choices. I believe effective helping involves making choices *with* others, and not *for* them. You have the freedom to choose for yourself. Even though life offers no guarantees or absolutes, you still need to make choices for yourself, and then live with the consequences of your choices.

When I hear people say, "I have to lose weight," I quickly make them aware of the fact that they don't *have to do* anything in life. Instead, I ask them if they *want to* control their eating. Wanting to do a task and having to do it hold two different psychological implications. Using such words as "have to," "should," and "must" implies you have no freedom of choice. Feeling as though you *have to* causes people to use some sort of self-punishment to motivate themselves to change. Self-punishing behavior only suppresses immediate actions; it does not work to create long-term positive changes. People who *want to* change are always much more successful than people who feel they *have to* change. Wanting to means you are looking forward to change and will use positive behavior to motivate yourself. By wanting to change, the motivation comes more from within, making it easier and more fun.

You choose whether to consider your weight problem the result of your genes, over which you have no control, or the result of learned patterns of behavior, over which you do have control.

Keep in mind that if the behavior is seen as learned, it can also be unlearned. Choosing to attribute the cause of your weight problem to something out of your control *allows you little room to help yourself*. Many of your choices directly contribute to your anxiety and frustration in life. If you unrealistically choose to lose twenty pounds in two weeks and fail, you feel frustrated and discouraged. You can't blame your genes for failing. But you can start making smaller, more positive choices for yourself that produce much more long-term change

"No kidding! So you were born with fat genes, too!"

than the bigger unrealistic choices that only produce anxiety and frustration.

WHAT SHOULD I DO?

Jim had been asking himself this for years. It wasn't until he started asking himself, "what do I *want* to do?"—not "what should I do"—that he began to feel good about himself and started losing emotional and physical weight. Jim's most frequently used word was "should," and he had strong justifications for why those "shoulds" should be.

Jim was always doing what he thought he *should* do, instead of what he *wanted*. He had created strong justifications making whatever he was doing seem worthwhile, because what he was doing in his life wasn't worthwhile in and of itself. Jim was always saying, "well, I should be a doctor—my father was," when he really wanted to be an engineer, or "I should be married and have a family," when in reality he was happy being single.

He thought his weight problem could be summed up in two words—ice cream. Yes, ice cream was certainly a factor in Jim's excess weight, but it wasn't the root of the problem. I pointed out to Jim that once he started to do what he *wanted* to do instead of what he felt he *should* do, he would lose *emotional* weight, and *physical* weight would naturally follow. Emotional weight would be lost because he would no longer be eating in response to the hidden frustration of not really being happy. Jim started to get to know himself by finally doing what he *wanted* to do. He began planning for a career in a field he truly loved instead of following someone else's rules.

The next time Jim came into my office he told me that he felt more motivated to lose his weight because now he *wanted* to be lean and healthy for himself instead of feeling that he *should* lose weight. After Jim lost his 15 pounds of excess body fat he realized how people are more successful when they really *want* to do something.

LEARNED HELPLESSNESS

All in all, it is up to you. You can choose either to sit by passively, feeling like a helpless victim, blaming your ancestor for not giving you the necessary genes, or you can choose to sit in the driver's seat and take control. You are not a helpless victim in life. Some people learn to be helpless.

Learned helplessness was studied in 1967 by Overmier and Seligman. In their study, dogs were placed in cages with no means of escaping, and given electrical shocks. Each time they were shocked and tried to escape, the dogs failed. After several trials the door of the cage was left opened and the dogs were again shocked. Even though they had a means of escape, the dogs never tried. The dogs learned and accepted being helpless. Think about it! This same concept could be applied to people who try one diet after another, or cling to an old approach to solving a problem, only to have it fail time and time again to control their eating. Eventually, these people will relinquish control, accept failure, feel helpless, and no longer try to achieve their goals, even though there is a successful and healthy way to do so. If you are like this, simply try a new approach, and get rid of the old approach that causes learned helplessness.

A new approach will give you a fresh start. If you are trying to be more positive and learn how to rebound from difficult problems, you don't keep rebounding back into the same old approach that doesn't help solve the problem. Granted, we are comfortable with the old approach because we are familiar with it, but it is just going to reinforce your feeling of helplessness. You are not helpless, but fully capable of making positive changes in your life that will help you overcome your eating problem.

Many behaviors and habits are learned. No one pops out of the womb yelling, "I believe in myself." Many of our inappropriate, unhealthy patterns of eating and thinking can be unlearned, while other appropriate healthy thoughts and behaviors can be learned, to establish a healthy mind and body.

DAVID

David had several behaviors to unlearn. David stood six feet two inches tall and had a little more than

100 pounds of excess body fat. He had scheduled an appointment with me only to call later and cancel because he had committed to being Santa Claus at his company's Christmas party. I later found this to be a common trait of David's—that he was constantly over-committing himself. When I asked David what he liked most about himself, he told me he was an extremely helpful and active person. Later, I discovered that he actually wanted to appear active only because he felt that most people viewed fat people as being lazy. Since David had such a low opinion of himself, he overcompensated by being "Mr. Helpful," always willing to lend a hand at the expense of fulfilling his own needs. He had been overweight for so long that he was really afraid of failure; the more afraid he was, the busier he became, in order to avoid having to face his weight problem.

David and I made an agreement, and set a goal that two days out of the week he would take time for himself and exercise. This was not an easy goal for David, since he had difficulty saying no to anyone asking for his help, and now had to face the risk of rejection. He began to realize that saying no to people could actually help them, especially in the case of his children, who relied too much on his help and needed to start taking some responsibility of their own.

David was amazed at how much body fat he could lose by simply skipping desserts at lunch and dinner. This sense of control created a feeling of hope for David. He started walking 30 minutes per day and started feeling stronger physically and mentally. He began paying more attention to good nutritional habits and cutting down on fats and sugar. David continued to work at expressing himself as he gained more confidence. I could always tell when David was doubting himself and his ability because he would once again become extra helpful, avoiding his own need to change. This was David's emotional weight, which kept him from losing physical weight. David continued to lose physical weight each week, allowing himself to adjust to both the physical and mental changes. The following Christmas David had to use a pillow to play Santa!

By learning to think more positively, you can make better choices for yourself. Once you experience some success from your choices, your whole life will change. You will become less critical and more trusting of yourself and others. This will then enable you better to control your eating, while accepting your mistakes and not being bound by them.

EXTERNAL VS INTERNAL CUES

I think most of you are now beginning to realize that weight control means a lot more than just losing some fat. It means more than what you see in the mirror or on the scale. Too much emphasis is placed on external cues like the mirror and scale. Not enough attention is placed on internal cues such as our thoughts—how we are feeling about ourselves. Ask yourself, "Why am I overeating? What am I looking for, and will I find it in the refrigerator?" Internal changes take place as you really get to know yourself. Beauty radiates from your newfound spirit of accomplishment and the feelings of success. If you spend as much time looking into yourself as you do looking in the mirror, you will find a great deal of beauty inside. Do you ever look in the mirror and say "Yuck! I look horrible and blimpy! I look like a rag, my hair looks terrible, I need a facelift, and a new life."? You get really nit-picky, finding fault with everything. Yet you don't really look any different from yesterday. What changed? It was your thoughts or attitudes about yourself. Don't you feel great even after just one day of eating healthily? Do you look different? No. You are feeling the beauty and pride of accomplishment.

Clearly, then, your thoughts reflect what you feel about yourself. So, the next time you pass the mirror, remember, *you are much more than just what is reflected in the mirror.* The positive reflection doesn't come totally from a new hair style or thinner body, but from the positive internal feelings about yourself.

JAN

Jan, age twenty-two, had about 35 pounds of excess fat to shed, and believed her *life* couldn't improve until her *thighs* did! Jan was usually very quiet and withdrawn in our counseling sessions, answering questions with a short yes or no, maybe a nod of her head and an "uhuh" occasionally. One day, she stormed into my office with great enthusiasm about her remarkable three-pound weight loss indicated by her bathroom scale. Jan proudly told me how people were treating her better, smiling at her, "Men were even looking at me!" Jan attributed this sudden change to the three-pound weight loss shown on the scale, which was an *external* cue. She didn't realize that her three-pound loss wasn't even noticeable. Actually, people were reacting to her newfound spirit of accomplishment, brighter smile, and sense of control—the *internal* changes.

GET RID OF THE SCALE: LISTEN TO YOURSELF

Do you use the scale as a way to seek approval? Not only do you look at the scale to tell yourself how you are supposed to feel, but you also use it as a private form of self-punishment. It usually starts when you overeat and then have such thoughts as, "Oh no! Here I go again, I have no willpower. I'll never be thin." You then step on the scale to support these negative thoughts and further punish yourself. I highly recommend that if you want to gain control over eating and your body weight, get rid of the scale and listen your own feelings. You can trust yourself! It doesn't matter what kind of eating problem you have, it is important to remember when you step on the scale that it doesn't tell you that you have emotional weight: ten pounds of anger about your body weight, and ooops ... about 5 pounds of guilt, etc. The scale doesn't make you aware of your emotional weight, it just makes you more frustrated and anxious, forming even more *emotional weight*. If emotional weight is not lost, the reason you were eating or not eating is still not dealt with. Eventually, your eating problem will return once again to provide you with a way to cope, and the refrigerator doesn't say *"close me and deal with your emotions!"* Maybe this phrase would be better to pin up on the refrigerator than a picture of some super sexy body of a stranger.

I have always disliked "before-and-after" pictures of people who lost weight. The "before" picture of Mary is taken when she's not wearing makeup, hasn't combed her hair, and is slouched over. On the "after" picture her makeup was done professionally, her posture has suddenly improved, and she holds her breath as they snap the picture! Now, here's Mary, she's thin but she still doesn't like herself; she still has that dead end job, and that crummy relationship. So when Mary looks in the mirror she's still not happy and she still thinks she's fat—thinking if she lost a few more pounds then she'd be happy. Once again she places that perfect picture on her refrigerator.

Don't rely on the scale to determine if your successful, or to provide you with a sense of accomplishment. It is not a good indicator. The scale tells you how many pounds you have lost, not fat. The scale may even show an increase because you have gained muscle by exercising. Muscle weighs more than fat. However, muscle takes up one-fifth the space of fat, resulting in inches lost; you will notice your clothes fitting better.

When you begin to notice on the scale that you are losing weight, the weight that is lost initially is not fat, but water and glycogen from your muscles and liver. Once your body begins to recognize that deficit in your caloric intake, it begins to fight back, in fear of starvation. *Your body* sees fat as survival, even though *you* see it as gross and ugly. This is usually seen by the dieter as the plateau period. The plateau period is the time when you're closer to losing fat than ever before—yet this is the time most people give up, or start severely restricting food, causing their body to fear starvation and hold onto fat. Start being kind to your body and preoccupied with how to eat healthily and keep motivated, instead of becoming preoccupied with the scale. The scale doesn't offer you any predictability; every day it can change, even for the healthiest person. You are the best indicator—*trust yourself!*

Decide today to start relying on internal cues—how you feel—while relying less on external cues. It's great when you get a compliment on how good you look, but the positive reinforcement is external, only helping you feel good about yourself for a couple hours. Then the excitement wears off and you need another external fix! By using internal controls, you and only you decide how you feel—not the scale or another person. When you look inside yourself, you'll see more hope for the future and answers to your problems. I'm sure you know the saying that what we are looking for is right under our noses. Yet we are always looking outside of ourselves for the answers, and by the time we ask five other people or spend thirty dollars on some miracle weight loss pill, we are even more confused and frustrated.

By using internal control, you can't say a person or event made you overeat or not eat. Take responsibility for your actions and thoughts. No one is making you think or act negatively. It's all in the way you perceive or label what has happened.

IT'S ALL IN THE PERCEPTION

A lot of what we experience in life is an act of perception and emotion. If you can't change prior happenings, you must control how you label or perceive what has happened. Learning to accept reality even when it gets pretty grim all depends on how you perceive what you are experiencing. You can perceive difficult times as a part of life that is necessary for positive growth, or you can see difficult times as the result of your stupid mistakes. Accepting reality means accepting the here and now, and focusing on the present. Focusing on the past just keeps you from living in and understanding the present. Many times the answers to our questions are in the here and now, and *what we do now determines our future.* The same applies to worrying about the future—it keeps you from *building* a future! Life is based in the present.

The negative thoughts you feed your mind create what I call negative labeling. The thoughts create positive or negative labels. It's the way you label yourself and the events in your life that affects the way you react! If you choose to label yourself fat, hopeless, weak, bulimic, anorexic, type A or B or C+, you begin to live up—or down—to those labels. Negative labeling can create or even worsen your feelings about yourself by causing a lot of anxiety and frustration. You can label failure as making you stronger and smarter or useless and stupid.

The thought that overcoming your eating problem is hopeless creates the *label* of helpless, and then you begin *acting* helpless.

Negative labeling is powerful! There is a difference between labeling an event impossible and labeling it difficult. If you label overcoming your eating problem impossible, you will no longer try to succeed. On the other hand, if you label it difficult, you'll continue to work toward overcoming it, and challenge those difficult

The way you label yourself is the way you will react.

times.   By labeling food good or bad, you give *food* power.   Labeling food bad makes you crave it more, always wanting the things you can't have.   Labeling cake "bad" makes you crave it; then once you eat this "forbidden" food you feel guilty, then the guilt leads to overeating, then to anger, frustration, and anxiety. Do you see how your overeating was triggered by both the way you labeled or perceived food, and then how it was further triggered by not listening to your emotions? The feeling of guilt was telling you to *stop,* and listen to yourself; there is something you're not understanding!

LABELING
food

ANXIETY
binging/purging
dieting/food restriction

GUILT
overeating
laxative use

FRUSTRATION

ANGER
self-punishing thoughts
disappointment in self

This same self-destructive cycle can be seen when a person steps on the SCALE.

STEPPING ON THE SCALE

WEIGHT GOES UP

EATING/BINGING/PURGING/FOOD
RESTRICTION/LAXATIVE USE GO UP

There is quite a big difference in the way people label things. For example, the word "elderly" means different things to different people. One person may label it THE END, while another labels it a wise and valued period in life, as in the Japanese culture. The same can be seen with the word "retirement"; it can be labeled as retiring from life, or as a beginning of a new chapter in life. Only you can decide. No matter what age you are, your happiness is still your responsibility. Strive to be happy!

There is also a huge difference between pain and discomfort when exercising. You will continue to exercise if you label what you are experiencing as "discomfort," not pain. This doesn't mean you should ignore what may be true pain. Pain is usually an indication that something is wrong. I suggest you get to know yourself and challenge your assumptions. Another example is the difference between hunger and appetite. Most of us have never really experienced hunger except for some severe cases of anorexia. Hunger is a physiological phenomenon, a sensation of weakness. There is a signal by the nerve impulses from the stomach to the brain and a drop in blood sugar, creating what is referred to as "hunger pangs." Appetite is a psychological phenomenon induced by smell, anger, boredom, or social situation, and many more reasons that will be explained later.

Quick assumptions and negative labels you choose to place on yourself provide excuses for not taking responsibility for making changes. If you label yourself hopeless, then why even keep trying? The majority of people entering my office have already placed negative labels on themselves. These negative labels and quick assumptions must be removed and replaced with positive labels and realistic, well thought through goals. Start really listening to yourself. The answers to all your questions lie within you. In counseling, I help people believe enough in themselves to *listen to themselves!*

JACK

Jack, a 33-year-old architect, was a well groomed, soft-spoken man whose physical weight seemed to settle in his protruding stomach. Jack avoided eye contact and spoke so softly that at times I had difficulty understanding him. One thing Jack did make clear was that he had labeled himself a person who lacked willpower, which was his reason for being overfat. Jack tried diet after diet and several diet pills in hopes of finding the willpower he was missing. He was searching for an easy way out, avoiding getting to the root of the problem. Jack didn't need diet pills to acquire willpower. He needed to take off the negative label of "lacking willpower" that he was using as an excuse. In psychology this is referred to as an *avoidance behavior.* Jack expressed that he was wishing I would tell him that he was a hopeless case, that I couldn't help him— he was too far gone. Sometimes, especially for Jack, it was easier to avoid facing things when reality got too painful to accept. Jack wanted to lose fat but didn't want to have to try very hard or for very long. He was carrying about 80 pounds of impatience, and as he became more patient he lost the *emotional weight* and the loss of physical weight followed.

ACQUIRING PATIENCE

Are some people just born more patient than others? Did the more patient people have mothers who stayed in labor longer, or did they have to wait longer to be fed as children? I don't think so! Usually, the patient person learned to be patient by realizing you get a lot farther in life that way. This doesn't mean being passive or lazy. But by being patient, you can become more successful without the anxiety and frustration that just make life more difficult. The key to freeing yourself from the anxiety of always having to start over is *patience.*

ASHLEY

At age 18, Ashley was suffering from burnout! She was always in a hurry and as a result never enjoyed what she was doing. Even when Ashley cried, she cried to a point of exhaustion. For the first few sessions, crying was about all Ashley could do, so I did most of the talking. However, this was okay because Ashley needed to cry to gain the control to be able to express her emotions. Some people think that crying is merely done by a person out of control. This is not true. Crying is done by people who are in control and it is for some people the preliminary to the expression of one's emotions.

Even Ashley commented on how good she felt after she cried—as if she had actually lost weight from crying. Ashley did lose weight, but it was not visible in the mirror's reflection. It was in her mind, in the form of *emotional weight*. In our sessions Ashley and I discussed her likes and dislikes, and what it felt like to be happy, and how she could deal with disappointments in her life. We discussed the importance of loving and being loved, as well as loving oneself. Talking about these feelings was new to her, and she said, "I didn't realize that it was okay to *feel*." After a while she began taking more time to *sit still* and get in touch with her feelings about what was happening in her life. She now realizes that we are not here just to perform a task in life, like some robot, and that through self-expression, life has much more meaning.

A few months after we had started counseling, Ashley reestablished her relationship with friends and family, realizing they were important people to her. She continued to use what she learned about nutrition by eating healthy, smaller, more frequent meals, realizing that food was not placed on this earth to punish herself with. Ashley lost 45 pounds of fat, through healthy eating, thinking, and regular exercising.

CHAPTER ONE: THINGS TO REMEMBER

* Just as food fuels the body, thoughts fuel the mind.

* Get rid of the scale, and get in touch with your feelings.

* Emotions were meant to be expressed.

* Food has no power but the power you give it.

* It is essential to understand the problems that cause eating problems—to deal with the causes, not the symptoms.

* Your thoughts—positive and negative—affect your body, and your chances of controlling your eating.

* Listen to yourself; *trust yourself.*

2

You're Only Human

We are all human, yet we seem to try so hard not to let anyone know it. As human beings, we allow ourselves little room for being human. We think of ourselves as having to be perfect—free of human error. Putting this kind of pressure on ourselves is self-destructive, and usually causes a fear of trying new things. It is easier to "play it safe" than make a mistake. People with eating problems foster an extraordinary fear of making mistakes, resulting in a need to *overcontrol* eating by restricting, binging, purging, or all three, creating what I refer to as a "personal power struggle." You want to develop *control* over eating—not *overcontrol*. Overcontrol comes from the fear of losing control, so you go to an extreme to prevent the possible loss of control. The irony of this is that control has already been lost. Diets and diet pills are both ways to place rigid perfectionist rules or restrictions on yourself, creating this overcontrol.

Not allowing yourself to be human produces the feeling of "If I can't do it perfectly, I just won't try." You then start to lose out on so much in life, by slowly losing more and more mental flexibility, becoming too afraid to experience anything new. Don't be afraid to make mistakes—try just being consistent, not perfect. Stop thinking that every time you make a mistake you have betrayed yourself in some way. Instead, realize that mistakes can actually be good for you. Mistakes keep you moving and working toward finding the answers to your problems. Mistakes keep you in the present, which is where the answers are, and your present actions determine your future. You do have control over the future, but dwelling in the past just stops you from living in the present which shapes your future! Ask yourself, "What is happening *now?*" Deal with your present situation!

It's up to you to choose to label your mistakes either as helpful or as an indication to quit. Was it the *mistake* that was so terrible, or was it the way you *reacted* to it? It is the mistakes that move you closer to your goals, and the excuses and self-punishment that are caused by needing to be so perfect that move you farther away. Mistakes are just part of getting started. This is why it is so difficult getting started, because it is when you make most of your mistakes. Learning how to make better choices for yourself requires making mistakes, which provides the opportunity to try a new direction.

ACCEPT YOURSELF

Accept yourself, and be yourself. It sounds simple, yet it does require obtaining insight into yourself. When I first counsel a client I may ask them what it is they want to achieve.

The most frequent response is "I guess what I want to change is ... oh ... just about everything about myself!" Most of the time these people don't need to change anything; instead they need to learn to accept themselves, and to learn from their mistakes is the first step. Could it be then, that mistakes are opportunities in disguise, helping us learn to accept ourselves? Insisting then on perfection makes accepting yourself difficult. Mistakes provide you with the opportunity to better yourself and to be yourself.

Accept yourself, and be yourself. To do this you must start to listen to yourself. Now this doesn't mean you analyze life, but live it! Really listen to your words, don't just say words. Your words reflect how you feel about yourself, which determines whether you will accept yourself, and therefore *be* yourself! Listen to your silent voice—that voice in your head that only you can hear. Is your silent voice harsh and rigid? Have you ever screamed at yourself in your mind? Start changing your silent voice, or silent words, to sound more kind and gentle. Maybe the solution to your headache isn't another aspirin, but a nicer, kinder voice. By listening to yourself you get more in touch with yourself, which enables you to better handle criticism. Listening to others also helps you look into yourself.

Mistakes can open you up to criticism and learning to handle criticism gives you insight into your values and beliefs. Constructive criticism is the way that a person expresses his or her feelings. Think about what the person has expressed, and ask yourself, "Has this given me any insight into myself?" If so, use it. If not, just let it go.

I also continue to hear people make comments like, "Opportunity only knocks once, so you'd better look hard and take what you can get or it will pass you by." With this kind of attitude people usually end up always waiting for that perfect time and perfect opportunity. Opportunity knocks millions of times in our lives, but too much of the time we are looking too hard and trying to be too perfect. No one can be a totally strong and perfect person and still be human. If you're not always in control, nothing terrible will happen. Relax! Opportunity knocks every time you make a mistake.

When you are growing and making changes in life is when you're the most vulnerable.

Individuals with eating problems believe that this feeling of vulnerability means being weak. Diets give support to this overly perfectionist, self-critical attitude by not allowing room for mistakes. "If you go off the diet, you were weak and you blew it!" Failure is not taken lightly by overly perfectionist, self-critical individuals, who usually resort to some form of self-punishment, like taking pills or laxatives, restricting, binging or purging food, and then—going on another diet. Opportunity is not a mystical or magical occurrence, but is brought about by being human and making mistakes while realizing that experiencing failure doesn't mean you can't succeed.

Success requires you to make a few mistakes, and to feel just about every emotion there is, before finding what is comfortable and works best for you. In my lectures, I often tell people to go out and try something new and take the chance of making a mistake, which can then be corrected. You can make a mistake and not lose your direction or control. Mistakes do not have to mean the end; instead, they can mean opportunity. If you happen to have an eating problem, you don't just let it exist; you learn to create a new strategy for self-control that is healthier. Mistakes are valuable learning experiences if you are to become *healthy, happy, and in control of eating.*

Millions of people who are thin are still not in control of eating, and their body weight is a struggling body weight. Not getting hung up on mistakes, and accepting them as a part of life, means that you are really accepting yourself as being human. In spite of your imperfections, you are an important person! So relax, and surrender all superhumanness: Stop trying so hard to be superhuman and be supersuccessful instead.

STRESS REDUCTION: LIGHTEN UP

When you lighten up mentally you'll lighten up physically. Taking the lighter approach means learning to deal with problems by relaxing, and reducing the stress that gets in the way of solving the problem. Stress is a part of the everyday process of living, and comes in many different forms. Relaxation and other stress reduction techniques are helpful in reducing the fear of dealing with problems. Bandura (1981) offered a theory of fear reduction using a direct and positive approach. He believed in bringing the fear to awareness *before* the situation arises. This way the clients get the message that they can do something about their distress or fear, rather than expecting no distress to occur. This expectation leads to more persistent effort to relax, and to more success, which further strengthens clients' sense of self-esteem. Then when a fear surfaces, clients have already dealt with the fear in their minds, and find the real situation easier to handle. This is an example of taking a lighter approach, done through awareness and relaxation techniques. The first step is to understand what stress is, and then to learn relaxation techniques through positive imagery similar to Bandura's concept.

There are several ways you can become aware of your own stress level. Stress affects everyone, and comes in many different forms. We are under stress every day, and sometimes the littlest thing can set us off. This is when we overreact to stress, especially when we are tired. We bring a great deal of stress on ourselves simply by our perceptions. Then there are those stresses caused by an illness, accident, loss of job, and even lack of exercise. Stress isn't always bad; it can motivate you to get a better job or to make other positive changes. There is good and bad stress. Good stress comes from getting a job promotion, buying a new car, or even going on a trip. This kind of stress is good stress, because you are in control of these experiences and they make you feel good. Bad stress makes you feel bad—out of control, helpless, and hopeless.

Bad stress shows itself when you just can't make up your mind about the simplest thing, or you start putting the cereal boxes in the refrigerator, or you chew six packs of gum in one hour. Have you chewed your nails down to nothing, and are now chewing on your pencil? Do your neck or shoulders feel stiff? Are you having trouble sleeping because thoughts pour into your mind when you try to relax?

Are you constantly saying to yourself, "I have too much to do"? If so, your body language is probably showing your frustration. Clinching your teeth, tapping your foot, gripping your hands, feeling nervous, and having headaches are all indicators of stress, which is worsened by turning to or away from food to reduce your frustration. Frustration can also come from a lack of challenge in life. Frustration is a form of bad stress.

If frustration is not overcome by creating a solution to the lack of time in your life, anxiety is the consequence. Anxiety and panic attacks affect millions and millions of people who have not learned these techniques for relaxing and lightening up. Relaxing and lightening up are part of overcoming the frustration, allowing you to find the solution. When you are all uptight you can't think straight. The pressure is too great to allow a creative thought for solving the problem to surface.

Have you ever had trouble remembering something, and the harder you tried the more frustrated you got? But the minute you said, "Oh well ... I'm sure I'll remember later,"—*Pop!*—the answer came to you. Why? Because you relaxed and allowed some creative thoughts to surface. This concept should be applied when trying to solve a problem: go take a walk or take your mind off the problem. The answer is there, you're just *trying too hard. Lighten up!* Here are some useful techniques you can use to lighten up, which serves two purposes:

(1) to relax, which immediately starts the process of reducing the stress from the anxiety, and (2) to start the creative process you need to solve the problem. Problems are solved not through logic, but through creative thought and self-expression. Expressing your feeling ensures you won't be holding stress for others. Just like there are hidden fats in foods, there are hidden stresses in people, and both are stored and built up in the body, affecting our health and well-being.

When you're all stressed out, creative thought is nowhere in sight! Ask yourself: "What thing do I do each day that I react to negatively that causes stress?" Then work at changing it. The work it takes to change it is far less stressful than letting the problem exist.

STRESS REDUCTION: LIGHTEN UP YOUR BODY (MUSCLE RELAXATION EXERCISES)

Find a quiet place. Lie on your back in a comfortable position, or sit comfortably, and close your eyes.

Begin by tensing your hands for five seconds and then relaxing them, letting them go limp. Think of your hands as being heavy and warm.

Then continue by moving up your body to forearm, upper arm, shoulders, neck, and jaw, first tensing them up for five seconds, and then working at making them feel loose and relaxed. To relax the jaw, open and close your mouth several times. When you are stressed out and anxious, grinding or biting down on your teeth is done unconsciously.

Be patient. It takes time to relax your body that has been stiff and tense all day!

Moving down now, tense up and then relax your feet and lower legs and upper legs.

Tell your body it feels relaxed!

When you begin to feel anxious or stressed out, *stop, tense up your muscles and then let them go.* Even if you

are at the office, this exercise could be applied successfully.

Continue on by tensing and relaxing your hips and
abdomen. Breath more from your diaphragm than from
your chest. This will help you breath slowly and more
naturally. When people get stressed, they breathe very
shallowly and without control.

Now let's continue by relaxing the mind.

LIGHTEN UP YOUR MIND
(MENTAL RELAXATION EXERCISES)

Close your eyes, and think of your forehead as cool.

Next, think of a passive statement: "Everything will
be just fine," or "I can and will make good choices for
myself. I trust myself." If any distressful thoughts enter
your mind, quickly say the word NO. Get rid of the
thoughts that make you stressed!

See the color blue in your mind. Blue is the color of
calmness and coolness. So visualize a blue sky or blue
water, while inhaling calmness or blue, and exhaling
tension and anxiety. Every time you exhale, think of it
as breathing away stress.

Bring into your mind some calming words: *love,
peace, happiness.* Repeat these words as often as you
want.

From now on talk softly to yourself in your mind.
Many of us are yelling at ourselves in our minds. Listen
to how you silently talk to yourself, and you'll understand how you are silently abusing yourself.

Be kind and compassionate to yourself!

IMPROVING SELF-ESTEEM:
BE KIND AND COMPASSIONATE TO YOURSELF

Another dangerous side effect to getting hung up on
mistakes is that it doesn't give you time to credit yourself for your successes. Put an end to always beating

yourself up mentally with harsh, punishing, negative silent words. This is *self-inflicted mental abuse*. Take out time to give yourself a pat on the back and a few words of praise. *Be kind and compassionate to yourself.*

Stop focusing your energies on what you believe are your weaknesses or limitations. Instead praise yourself for showing the smallest improvement. By acknowledging accomplishments, your self-esteem will increase and you'll become more internally motivated.

I constantly hear the phrase: "A person must love themselves first." This phrase always confused me. How do I love myself—do I walk by the mirror and throw myself a kiss, or hug myself? Obviously not. So what does it mean, and how do you love yourself? Everything we have been talking about so far is the process that leads you to loving yourself. Loving yourself means being kind to yourself, and by acknowledging your accomplishments you are giving yourself and what you do in life value. A person with "no value" has low self-esteem. During counseling, we take out time to acknowledge accomplishments and talk about how these accomplishments make people feel, and how they help with making future goals easier. This is called self-exploration—exploring yourself and building a strong positive identity. Loving yourself means feeling good about your morals, values, attitudes, beliefs, accomplishments—even mistakes. Be proud of being you!

Give yourself value by exploring yourself. To attain a healthy body weight, you need to have a healthy mind and body as well as to love yourself enough to want to work hard at overcoming your eating problem. It is *your* life. Work hard to make it better, and don't be so quick at giving in to old destructive habits.

If someone were physically punching you in the arm over and over again until you bruised, you would fight back, defending and taking care of yourself. Yet, by hanging on to your eating problem you continue to hurt yourself *physically* by poor eating habits, and *mentally* by beating up on yourself with your silent abusive words. Please don't dump on yourself. Be kind and compassionate to yourself.

VICKI

When Vicki entered the office she headed right toward the couch and sat down. Vicki was a beautiful 26-year-old woman who was at an unhealthily low weight. She was binging and purging and then starving herself. She had dark circles under her eyes and looked malnourished. Vicki complained that she had trouble thinking straight and was tired all the time.

I asked her how she was feeling and she immediately started crying. As strange at it may sound, I was happy to see her cry, because it meant she was allowing herself to feel her emotions.

The Kleenex box can be a good friend, and was especially so for Vicki. She continued to cry as she painfully told me how she felt confused and frightened, and that she had not done anything with her life. She was extremely self-critical and was obsessed with food and overexercising, and was starting to miss days at work. She told me at first these activities made her feel good and in control, but now she hated herself and felt out of control. Vicki said, "When I weigh myself the scale shows that I'm losing weight, but I feel heavier now than 20 pounds ago."

When I asked her how many calories she was consuming, she said that since she was so afraid of food she didn't want to keep track of calories. She admitted that she went for days without eating and then would binge and purge. She began making small changes, such as eating breakfast and remembering to eat smaller, more frequent meals in order to stay alert. Eventually, I had her bring her lunch and I saw how fearful she was of eating. While she was eating she showed no enjoyment, and tried desperately not to lose control. She told herself she didn't like food, because if she liked food she won't be able to stop eating. I was very happy with Vicki's attempt at eating.

Vicki told me she had been hospitalized two years ago and had to undergo hyperalimentation. (Hyperalimentation is the administration of a greater than optimal amount of nutrients done intravenously using a catheter inserted through the superior vena cava.) This gave Vicki 2,200 calories daily. She told me she began to eat because everyone wanted her to, and it was the only way to get out of the hospital so she could start restricting food again. This was Vicki's master plan, and she focused all her mental energy on eating and fooling the doctors and her family into thinking she was better.

Vicki was never kind to herself and felt nothing she did was good enough. God himself could have come down and told her that she couldn't have done it better, and she still wouldn't be satisfied. Together we worked at slowing down and on acknowledging her accomplishments. Even after our first session she felt better about not having to deal with her fears alone. Each session brought to mind a new awareness of her values, attitudes, and beliefs, and as she started to explore who she was she actually *liked* who she was.

She had to slow down and take a look at herself. She was moving too fast. I told her if she was driving and needed to see the address on the house she would have to slow down, otherwise she would just keep on passing it, thinking that the house wasn't there. I began to educate her in the basics of nutrition, and invited her to give a small presentation at one of my lectures. I believe that the better people understand something, the more they can believe and the more likely they will conquer it. Nutrition began to interest her, and so did helping others, and she enrolled in a local college.

Every time I met with Vicki I could tell she was growing stronger and gaining a positive self-esteem. At our last session, she came in looking rather solemn and told me she finally realized that it wasn't food or her fear of fat, but rather the fear of not being perfect. But now, perfect was out, being herself was in. She had had more fear of making a mistake and of failure than she did of food.

This realization didn't come overnight. Vicki had to work hard and face things that she could have avoided by focusing on food and physical weight. If she would have given up in a couple of weeks these insights never would have been realized.

Was losing weight the solution to Vicki's problems? No. Obviously, a person's low self-esteem is not stored in their fat cells but in their minds. The scale doesn't tell you that you have about 10 pounds of anger and about 20 pounds of guilt and 15 pounds of boredom. So losing fat doesn't mean you lose these feelings about yourself. Even once you lose physical weight you are still going to be you, so you'd better start liking who you are inside or the outside will never be good enough or thin enough.

DON

About a year ago I counseled an attractive 26-year-old man named Don. He was about 55 pounds overfat and had a very low self-esteem. His low self-esteem (emotional weight) showed itself by his fear and resentful feelings about people, and by his belief that people were always criticizing him. Even when people complimented Don on how good he was looking, he *perceived* what was said as meaning that he was looking fatter. As he engaged in self-exploration and started being kind to himself, realizing his value as a person, he came to like himself. He didn't change physically, but emotionally. As he better understood himself, his perceptions of how others saw him became positive. He said, "I feel lighter but the scale is the same; something must be wrong with it." Don was trusting his own perceptions even more than the scale, and he happily got rid of it, adding more space to his bathroom! This change in emotions led to physical loss of fat as his belt buckle had to be moved over several inches.

Don learned to expand his psychological life so that he became less preoccupied with food. He stopped dieting and learned to eat healthily. I believe that the more Don avoided food, the more he learned not to trust himself. His mistrust in himself was reinforced when he would eat "forbidden" foods, which made him feel like he was weak and couldn't be trusted around food; he would then deprive himself of food. Don also felt that everyone thought he was weak because he was so fat, and that they didn't know that he could be strong enough not to eat any food for days. Not eating is supposed to be a sign of strength and willpower, yet it only makes you weaker and more obsessed with food. Not eating shows fear and lack of trust in oneself, not strength. Eventually, Don realized these were his own feelings, and not those of others. He also learned that the more he deprived his body the more it fought back by converting and storing as fat the little amount of food he was eating. His body was fearing starvation, and the more he restricted food the fatter he got.

Maybe you are saying, "Oh, *wow*, this could be me, and I never knew this was why I never lost weight even when I was eating nothing." Now, when Don learned this about the body, he really changed his way of eating. He stopped dieting, and he stopped thinking that not eating was the answer. What about you? Will you take this information and make a change, or will you just continue on with the same old approach that has been keeping you miserable, in hopes that your body is

different than the rest of the people on the planet earth?
Think about this for a moment. What if I were to give
you a loaf of bread and tell you this was all the food you
were going to get for two weeks? What would you do?
Would you eat the whole loaf in just a couple of days, or
would you save it and use it slowly until more food was
available? You bet, you would use it sparingly! Just
like your body saves food and fat when it is not getting
enough food. Your body is smart and saves fat just like
you saved the bread. I hope you use this information
like Don did.

FOCUS ON THE PROCESS

Focus on the process and not the end goal. If all
you are concerned about is losing 30 pounds, then your
10 pounds will never be recognized as an accomplishment. You'll find yourself saying, "So what if I lost 10
pounds; I've got 20 more to lose." With this kind of attitude, you'll end up gaining the 10 pounds back. Some
goals are better accomplished by not focusing on the
end goal, but by keeping in your mind that the *process*
will without a doubt get you to your goal! By focusing
on the process you give each day your very best, and
don't worry about the end goal. You'll get there! In
your daily process, practice being patient and flexible.
Don't say, "I'll never have another cookie, beer, or glass
of wine"—remember, you are only human. The word
"never" is stress-producing, as well as unrealistic and
inflexible, leading only to short-term changes and a lot
of wasted energy. Have you ever noticed how you may
still have energy even after working hard because you
feel so good about what you did? Maybe one of the reasons you feel tired is because you don't feel good about
what you are doing, or should I say *not* doing!
When you are flexible you develop better coping
ability and no longer turn to or away from food for

comfort and control. You may sometimes feel as though you are trapped in your body, but you are really trapped in your inflexible, rigid demands.

These feelings of entrapment grow as you become more impatient about getting to the end goal and then start to hurry a process that can't be hurried. Saying you'll never binge or purge again causes enough stress to make you binge even sooner. Eliminate the word "never" from your vocabulary and you will eliminate both physical and emotional weight.

Day-to-day goals are easier than setting your sights on a three- to four-month goal that distracts you from seeing your daily progress. Three- to four-month goals usually become one- week goals when you don't see your progress fast enough, expecting too much too soon. As a result, emotional weight (frustration, anxiety) goes up, and physical weight will go up through overeating or down through restriction of food. By looking at the process, you can stay reinforced longer by giving yourself praise for day-to-day accomplishments. If you are planning to go to Hawaii and expect to lose 20 pounds in one week, remember, your body doesn't care if you are going to Hawaii, and it has several well designed mechanisms that will fight your starvation diet. You can only override your psychological and physical need to eat for a short time, which usually ends in binging. The more you restrict food, the more your body fights back. People have asked me to give them some sort of pill to repress their appetite because they are always hungry, as they stand there looking sick and weak. Being hungry is part of survival. If this mechanism weren't there you would die. So listen to your body and learn the difference between emotional and physical hunger. *Both* are mechanisms to help you.

Always trying to lose weight for a temporary situation always results in temporary change, by putting you back on the roller coaster of losing, gaining, eating or not eating, hating yourself, or liking yourself. Laxatives

Dieting is a vicious cycle with no beginning or end. You're always starting over!

and appetite suppressants, are short-term solutions to what will continue to be a long-term problem if you don't take a healthier direction. One of the most beautiful rewards of overcoming any eating problem is the beauty of accomplishment, as you remember the time you could have binged or purged but instead you dealt with the guilt or anxiety causing it. Perhaps instead of overeating because of boredom, you changed those uninteresting thoughts and actions to something more challenging. Instead of satisfying your taste buds you are satisfying your mind! If you had used diet pills, you'd always feel that it wasn't you that succeeded, but the pills; you'd never feel the beauty of accomplishment—just more disillusionment. Trying to control physical weight through restricting food gives you an empty feeling, both physically and psychologically.

JASON

Jason, age 40, father of three, joined the program after seeing several of his friends achieve their ideal body weight. When he first joined my program, he was very skeptical and nervous about not being on a "diet." Jason could not comprehend how he could lose physical weight without dieting. He was extremely preoccupied with food and the scale, weighing himself after each meal. He kept a scale in his filing cabinet next to his health food potato chips! We made sure that he got rid of the key to that cabinet.

Jason started focusing on watching other changes, like getting stronger or increasing his mental endurance. He had spent the majority of his life in a state of constipation and gas. For the first time in years his system was regulated, and he was losing inches, through moderation—not through sacrificing all the foods he enjoyed. Jason learned the difference between emotional hunger and physical hunger. The potato chips represented his emotional hunger: when things at the office got busy, anxiety increased, and so did Jason's eating. While eating the potato chips helped him deal with the stress of the office, later he had to deal with the stress of the office and indigestion! Things just backfired, getting worse.

Jason took things a step at a time. He realized that he was in control of eating, that food had no power but the power he was giving it, and that using food for emotional support gives it power. The potato chips were being used for emotional support (reducing his anxiety), and now that he had found a healthier way to deal with his anxiety, he didn't eat the chips.

Jason later told me, "I'm going to give healthy foods the power to make me feel better." He no longer stepped on the scale. He also realized he was using the scale to tell him just how long could he eat junk food before the scale would go up. If the scale didn't go up he thought, "Good, I can keep eating like this." Now he knows that gaining weight is just one of the hundreds of dangerous side-effects developed from junking out! When the scale went up he always felt tired and weak, but instead of focusing on these feelings the scale distracted him from listening to himself. Jason's last words to me were, "I did it without dieting." His eating program was tailored for his individual needs, which gave him a large variety of foods, never creating the feeling of self-deprivation.

ANDREA

I also recall a young woman named Andrea, age 29, coming to my office for the first time. With her head bent down, and breathing very nervously, as she kept on repeating, "I don't know what's wrong! I don't know what's wrong!" Andrea was of normal body weight and had apparently lost 45 pounds by using laxatives and appetite suppressants. Even with this considerable weight loss she had not yet begun to feel good about herself. She felt something was missing. We later discovered it was her sense of control that was missing.

Andrea didn't feel she had lost the weight, but rather that the laxatives and pills were responsible for her success. She continued to use these pills and feared what would happen if she stopped.

Even after losing her weight, over two years ago, Andrea's dependence on these drugs was her way of masking the fear of losing control and regaining her weight. She felt unable to handle events that she used to handle with ease; the laxatives and pills had taken their toll on her emotionally and physically. Her hair was dry and brittle, her skin had turned rough and flaky, and she was constantly tired and rundown. As I counseled Andrea, she told me how she didn't feel good about herself, and how she had thought that once she was thin she would automatically like herself. She described herself as a high achiever who was frequently disillusioned because she had a tendency to set unrealistic expectations.

I've talked with numerous people like Andrea who felt that once they were thin all personal insecurity, uncertainty, and low self-esteem would simply melt away along with fat. Her fat was gone, but her problems were still waiting to be solved.

After several months of counseling, Andrea rid herself of the destructive drugs, and became aware that she was in control only when she trusted herself. She chose to put the drugs into her mouth. Most of all, Andrea came to understand that her weight wasn't the cause of her problems, but merely the symptom, and the drugs were used as a distraction to avoid dealing with the problems.

MARTHA

Another client who faced problems similar to Andrea's was a young woman, Martha, a 19-year-old college student who had lost 36 pounds in two months.

Martha had a bony appearance and was obviously underweight. Her clothes hung on her small frame as she told me how heavy she felt. Martha cried frequently during our sessions, expressing constant disappointment in herself. She stated that, "All the clothes I try on make me look fat!"

Martha's mental changes hadn't met with her physical changes, and she still felt fat, but it was in her mind, not her body. Martha told me if she ever stopped counseling with me, she would start binging and purging to lose weight. She continued to indirectly threaten me with the possibility that she might become bulimic. In other words, she was trying to tell me she felt out of control and needed help. Both Martha's and Andrea's behaviors were inconsistent with their attitudes, so they were now trying to change either the behavior or the attitude that was causing unpleasant feelings about themselves. Andrea's belief that taking drugs was not healthy conflicted with her feeling that she needed them for weight control. This was Andrea's coping mechanism. Martha's belief that losing more weight would solve her problems conflicted with her feelings that she was already too thin.

In psychology we call this occurrence *cognitive dissonance*. This is when there is an uncomfortable psychological state in which the person experiences two incompatible beliefs. Cognitive dissonance is something all of us experience when trying to make a decision. For the first two weeks of counseling, Martha was too afraid to begin eating more food, so we began to engage in self-exploration, bringing her to the awareness that her fear wasn't about getting fat, but about trusting herself.

Both these women were normal, healthy people who began like many do, by simply going on a diet that preoccupied their minds. Many severe eating problems start with focusing on dieting in hopes of shedding a few pounds.

FINDING A PURPOSE

Another interesting stress producer is the way we label the *reason* we want to lose weight. I have noticed a remarkable difference in stress levels between people who label their reason for weight control as a means only to improve their appearance, and the people who label their reason for weight control as a means to improve their health. When the purpose was for appearance's sake only, people exhibited, to a great extent, more stress than did the people whose purpose was to control weight for health reasons. Why? It appears that people losing weight only to improve their appearance compared themselves to others more frequently, feeling more competitive. They also had higher feelings of inadequacy about themselves, feeling self-critical, producing an enormous amount of stress. This is especially prevalent in anorexia and bulimia, where people with these problems are constantly comparing themselves to others, believing others to be thinner than themselves. Most of us do, however, overestimate our own bodies and underestimate the body size of others, just as we usually give others more credit for their accomplishments even when we perform the same task, a behavior seen more in appearance-conscious people. On the other hand, losing weight for the purpose of improving health meant little competition with others and fewer feelings of inadequacy. These people were not as self-critical, and therefore exhibited a great deal less stress. The less-stressed people also showed a lower frequency of overeating, or restriction. There is a lot of power that comes from the way we label ourselves and our purpose for our goal. As we all know, many of us eat as a way to reduce stress, but overeating doesn't give us the inner satisfaction we need.

Another finding showed that appearance-conscious people seemed to depend more on others, as well as the scale and mirror (external cues), for reinforcement, and were more apt to blame others and to blame events (external cues) for lack of success with weight control. In comparison, health-conscious people who were more independent in their reinforcement needs proved to be more internally motivated by feelings of renewed strength, flexibility, lightness, or a greater range of motion. They depended little on others for positive reinforcement. Don't misunderstand me; there is nothing wrong with needing some positive reinforcement, inspiration, and guidance from others, because we can learn a lot from other people.

We need to compare ourselves to others as a way to better understand ourselves and our purpose. In time of need, getting an honest opinion from someone you respect is a wonderful idea. It is when you take it too far and need others to stay motivated and provide you with a sense of identity that it is an unhealthy dependency. Have you noticed how a complement is very short-lived, and usually keeps you motivated for about an hour? When you depend totally on others for reinforcement, you are taking the chance that your support system may not always be there. There is also the chance you'll start doing what other people want and not what you want. When this happens, you can become a *people pleaser.* Your self-esteem is based on making everyone else happy, while *you* are miserable. This also puts a lot of stress on others, who feel they have to keep you feeling good.

I believe that learning and finding a purpose go hand in hand. Finding a purpose can occur in many ways, through self-talk, or by talking with others, or even by learning through observation—and, of course, through action. You may also need to stop comparing what you think of as your bad points to others' good points. This is a very common thing to do.

Being internally motivated doesn't mean you don't need people. When you are internally motivated it requires less effort to make changes, because you are not looking for a reward or social approval, just *your own* approval. Making the change is for your own sake and your own desire. The more you make changes in this way, the less approval and reinforcement you will need.

Finding your purpose is easier when you develop good associations with people who have similar goals. However, each of us may use a different approach because our thoughts and actions motivate us in different ways. So you can use others' experiences as stepping stones to better understand what works best for you.

Your behavior is directed toward the attainment of a purpose, for yourself or another person. Find your purpose and set your goals. Having a purpose serves as a source of motivation, meaning your purpose stimulates action. You know that to keep your job you have to get up in the morning and arrive at work on time. Your job allows you to fulfill several purposes, which motivates you to keep it. You don't get a paycheck (external motivator) every day, do you? Still, you go to work knowing that in two weeks you'll get paid. Even though your boss may not thank you for coming into work each day or constantly tell you what a wonderful employee you are, you still go to work. You found a purpose for going to work and learned how to keep yourself internally motivated, while you wait for your paycheck. To overcome an eating problem you must find your purpose. Once your purpose is established, becoming internally motivated follows, as you create a strong link between purpose and action. Just like going to work, there are days you don't want to go, and there will be days you don't feel like sticking with your goals needed to overcome your eating problem. This is when you once again *commit yourself to your purpose with determination.*

WHAT'S WRONG WITH ME?

What's wrong with you? There is nothing wrong with *you*. What's wrong is your *approach*. You need to try a new approach and to stop clinging to the old approach that hasn't worked. Trust yourself enough to take a new approach! The old approach to overcoming your eating problem always has you starting over again, making you feel like a failure; it slowly chips away at your self-esteem. Developing a positive self-esteem is as important as developing healthy eating habits.

To find what approach works best for you, step outside yourself. I don't mean you're supposed to have some cosmic experience. I mean examine your attitude and pretend you are counseling a friend and he or she is telling you their problem. It always seems to be easier to solve others' problems because we have more objectivity, and this is a way you can create your own.

If a friend came to you and said they were restricting food for days, or purging, you wouldn't tell them that it was fine and a great way to cope with problems or control weight. What *would* you tell them?

When trying a new approach, start out slowly. If not, you'll run out of steam, and burn out. There is always a little healthy anxiety that exists when just taking a new approach, which can sometimes lead to moving too fast because you are anxious. Slow down and relax. No need to rush. If you rush you will become frustrated. As emotional weight goes up, eating goes up and physical weight returns. Many times you may even find that as emotional weight goes up eating and physical weight will go down as you get thinner. But the emotional weight keeps you feeling heavier, so you further restrict food to lose that heavy feeling.

Diets move us farther from meeting our needs and getting to the root of the problem, because you are starving yourself physically and mentally as the association between food and guilt grow stronger.

This can also lead to punishing yourself for being overweight, anorexic, or bulimic, as the guilt about who you are and what you are doing create in your mind about 200 pounds of emotional weight.

ENERGY ZAPPERS!!

Energy zappers leave you feeling tired, zapping you of hope and motivation! Dwelling on what you have already done is just a form of silent self-punishment and energy zapping, only moving you farther from your purpose, and causing more unhappiness and fatigue. People who dwell on the negative are "if only I could have" people. "If only I could have said no to the hot fudge sundae, I wouldn't have binged" or "If only I were thin, then I would be happy," or "If only I had Tom Selleck or Victoria Principal in my life, then I'd be happy." If-if-if-if-if; rather than "if-ing" your life away, ask yourself "What can I do now to make things better?"

When you continue to challenge yourself and ask "What can I do to help myself?" your mind begins to search for solutions—immediately giving you energy. Whereas, the "If only I would have," attitude leaves you full of regrets, with no solution in sight. Dwelling on the negative gives you a way to avoid making positive changes. If you dwell on the past you never have to face the future and any further disappointments. But you'll also never get to the root of your eating problem.

Worrying about what hasn't happened yet is another energy zapper. You're tiring yourself out before you've gotten started by focusing on disaster. I do realize why you are thinking this way, and I'm sure you have good reason, especially if this is your tenth attempt at trying to overcome your eating problem. However, realize also that this is only hurting you and making it even harder to get started for the eleventh time. If you're already predicting disaster you'll never get started. It is amazing how we have such a good memory for our negative experiences and such a poor memory for the positive ones. I'm sure there were some positive experiences in between that you could now focus on to bring about a feeling of hope and renewed energy. Take even the smallest positive experience and blow it up—just like you used to do with the negative. If I were to say to you, "You've got a great personality, you're beautiful, talented, need to lose a few pounds, you're a creative and giving person," what did you remember most? That's right—"you need to lose a few pounds." What happens even to the best worker whose boss calls him or her into the office? Does he think, "Oh great, I'm getting a raise," or does he think, "Oh no, what did I do wrong?" Don't zap yourself by saying, "Oh well, here I go again, trying to overcome my eating problem, and I'll probably blow it!" Instead say, "I'm going to learn from my past experiences, not regret them!" If you do this you won't find yourself later saying, "See—I knew I'd blow it."

Don't worry about what hasn't happened yet and eliminate the if's and the dwelling on the past or worrying about the future, because it only keeps you from living in and changing the present. Dwell on what you *want* to be—healthy, happy, and in control of eating.

SHELLY

I remember counseling Shelly, a 21-year-old college student, who had a habit of always eating alone. She would wait until everyone was sleeping and engage in late-night eating with Johnny Carson. As soon as Ed McMahon said, "Heeeere's Johnny," Shelly would automatically prepare to have dinner with Johnny, usually emptying the contents of the refrigerator. Shelly was very comfortable with this routine and remarked how Johnny never told her she was getting heavy. Shelly began to make small changes, such as having dinner with Johnny only twice a week. The rest of the week she had dinner with her family, sitting at a table, eating in front of people. Shelly was very uncomfortable around food and even more so eating in front of people. Her awkwardness at eating in front of people was due to her feeling that she shouldn't be eating because she was overweight. While she may sound like a person who was severely overweight, Shelly had approximately 20 pounds of physical weight and 100 pounds emotional weight. Shelly took a couple of months to totally feel comfortable with eating in front of people, as she learned the importance of eating and nutrition. Shelly had previously viewed food as "destructive calories" and now saw it for what it was—nutritional fuel for the body. Shelly still watches Johnny Carson every night, but now invites her family to join her, realizing that conversation is both enjoyable and noncaloric.

HABITS AND BEHAVIORS

To permanently overcome your eating problem, you need to better understand your behaviors and habits. This is done by bringing them into awareness and then taking the necessary steps to break unhealthy habits, replacing them with new healthy behaviors. You may be wondering what the difference is between a behavior and a habit. A *habit* is something you do almost spontaneously, and sometimes may not even be aware you are doing it—like eating a bowl of potato chips while watching television, or nibbling on the food you are preparing for dinner—devouring a full dinner before dinner—and then wondering why you are not losing physical weight.

A few more examples would be the purging of food. It becomes an unhealthy habit that needs to be brought into awareness. It is like many habits that seem vitally necessary until replaced with healthy behaviors. The cigarette smoker who lights up another cigarette while three are already burning in the ashtray may strongly deny that those cigarettes were his. Smoking is a habit, and eating problems also can become habits. For the

The more we deprive ourselves, the more we learn not to trust ourselves. What are you really looking for?

cigarette smoker who always reaches into the right-hand pocket of his shirt for a cigarette, putting the cigarettes in his left-hand pocket makes him aware that he is taking another cigarette, changing his habit to a behavior.

A *behavior* is something you are more aware of.

Once a habit becomes a behavior you can better control it, because now you are aware of it. Do you have the habit of opening and closing the refrigerator fifty times—even after you know there is only some bread and pickles inside? Do you find yourself doing this even after a full meal? What are you looking for? Ask yourself if this is a physical hunger or an *emotional* hunger ? If you find yourself eating and eating but never feeling satisfied, it is an *emotional* hunger. Break this habit by asking yourself, "Am I thirsty?" Many times you may be mistaking thirst for hunger, or being tired for hunger. Do you feel guilty and ashamed if you eat dessert or one of your "forbidden" foods in front of people? Do you feel that eating these foods would mean you're weak and vulnerable—and that not eating means you're being strong? This is an unhealthy mental habit, because you later find yourself sneaking into the kitchen when everyone is in bed and eating six pieces of dessert instead of the one piece you would have eaten at the table. Break this habit, and be strong and eat a piece of dessert at the table with other people, changing your unhealthy habit to a healthy behavior. Eating dessert isn't what makes you feel bad. It is the way you hide what you are doing that makes you feel bad—bad enough to overeat or purge. Yet you place all your bad feelings onto food. What about the habit of walking into the kitchen immediately upon coming home, or the habit of eating every night around 10:00 when you are *tired,* not hungry. There is nothing wrong with eating a *healthy* snack before you go to bed, because it keeps you burning calories as you sleep. This occurs because your body is using energy to digest, assimilate, and transport the nutrients from the food. Try eating a rice cake with fresh-ground peanut butter, with no salt or sugar added. Don't say, "I can't control myself around peanut butter." Try waiting 15-20 minutes before you eat, and ask yourself if your hunger is coming from the anticipation about the approaching day?

Do you feel anxious, frustrated, or angry about your job? Are you feeling frustrated because you didn't have enough time to finish your work? Possibly, you're tired and need to slow down and rest—not just fall into bed and then not be able to sleep. Food has no power but the power you give it.

If you have a food allergy or need to avoid food containing molds, like peanut butter, you can have some sunflower or pumpkin seeds, or an apple. Just stay away from binging at any time of the day or night. Try having a glass of water with lemon or a warm cup of tea. The more you tell yourself you can't eat at night, the more you're going to eat. Listen to yourself. There is nothing wrong with eating foods at any time of the day as long as it is a *physical* hunger not an *emotional* hunger.

Get in tune with your natural body drives, rather than fighting them. Listen to them. This will be fully explained in the next chapter. Overcoming your eating problem means you really get to know yourself. It is a good experience that increases self-awareness. Habits are challenging to break because they fit so nicely into your life and have become routine. You have accumulated many habits, good and bad, over the years, and therefore you may find there is little room to bring in new behaviors. Healthy behaviors, once they begin to fulfill your needs, then become healthy habits. This requires giving our new healthy behavior time to work. Be patient—it's a good habit.

WEEKEND BINGING

Another unhealthy habit is weekend binging. You do great all week and something strange happens to your control on the weekend. Maybe a full moon? No, it is much simpler than that. One reason for weekend binging is the lack of structured time you are so used to during the week. To break the weekend habit of eating, you need to form a more structured time, by creating ways to relax, not by turning to or away from food for comfort and relaxation. Plan your activity and foods you will eat for the next day. Don't spend your weekend snuggled close to the refrigerator. Call a friend get a little sunshine. Don't just say, "There is nothing for me to do." Use your creative energy and make some decisions. Don't just pretend to be a helpless victim of the weekend. If you are bored, change your thoughts and actions to something more exciting. Start living life. Each weekend you make good healthy changes, take out time to reward yourself psychologically and physically with healthy foods. Taking care of your body is the way you should reward yourself. Say to yourself, "I did good last weekend. That means this weekend will even be easier."

WANTING TO CHANGE

The most important point here is that to break a habit you need to want to change. If you don't want to change you'll stay exactly where you are. The willingness to change is a part of overcoming your eating problem. Telling some people that they need to want to change terrifies them. They'll say, "Oh, wait a minute, you mean I need to make time to exercise, eat right and change my thinking ... It's just not the right time." So back to the diets and self-punishment, instead of making these changes a step at a time. There is never a perfect time, but the present is the right time.

Since we realize that the quick weight loss diets and pills, as well as food restriction, binging, and purging, do not work, why do so many people keep on using them? The more tired and hopeless they become, the more power people give these gimmicks and methods. You burn out by using more energy to continually deal with the disappointment from using these methods than you would have by making positive changes. Psychologically, when you get tired you'll always search for an easy way out—like the ever popular creams that will magically melt away fat after just one application. Then of course, there's the rubber suit that peels off pounds as you prepare to enter outer space, or should I say to leave the context of reality! It is the belief in the gimmick that makes the gimmick work for that one week. So why not get rid of the gimmick and start believing in yourself? Even after using all these gimmicks you still don't end up looking like the man or woman on the cover of the magazine. You are a unique individual physically and emotionally, and you must learn to focus on your best qualities and to accept yourself.

Remember, losing fat results in the loss of fat, not identity. Start right now, by being the best you can be, and don't wait until you're at your ideal body weight to express your personality. Let others get to know you. If you decide to isolate yourself from establishing a relationship or enjoying life, it will make overcoming your eating problem much more difficult. Later, you may even find yourself unhappy and resentful toward people who you believe like you now, because you are thin. Why didn't they like you before? Get out there and interact with people and you'll realize people like you better when you like yourself.

I know these changes are difficult and frightening, but they are possible. To some extent we all can get comfortable with the way things are, even if they're not good. We get stuck in the daily routine of paying the bills, going to work, and watching TV, or thinking the same thought through 600 times. This is when we are simply existing, not living, and we forget about happiness and being satisfied. Emotional weight goes up as fear becomes anxiety and eventually depression. This is how a problem becomes extremely complicated, by emotions building up and mixing up. While a certain amount of predictability and responsibility in our lives is necessary, we may find ourselves falling into a familiar rut. Change may be frightening because it is not necessarily predictable and it is usually filled with uncertainty. Change will always be somewhat frightening because there are no guarantees or absolutes in life.

Each time you change, you take a risk. But each change helps you believe more in yourself and your potential. Only you have the power to change.

I can't, and never will, have the power to change anyone but myself. I help people learn to listen to themselves and then believe enough in what they hear to make a positive change. Change also occurs much more easily when we can relax and no longer look at life in a black or white framework. Things are not just good or bad, happy or sad, but involve a little of both. Viewing life in such a rigid, cut-and-dried manner does not allow for being human. Thinking of yourself as either good or bad with no "middle ground" means that if you're not good, then you must be bad, or if you're not happy, you must be sad. Having the middle ground means that you can still be satisfied, content, somewhat happy, and just okay. You can be somewhat good if you only ate two brownies, instead of your usual six. Even in this situation, acknowledging your improvement over a past behavior is crucial to staying motivated.

Living life to such extremes is *extremely stressful*. You may not realize you possess such a rigid attitude. Yet you frequently question why you don't feel good, happy or energetic about life. You must change your black-and-white look at life. Sometimes, you won't do good or bad with your eating but "all right." Accept this as okay, and keep on going. Be kind to yourself and don't be so quick to label yourself and events so rigidly. Don't forget the lighter approach.

Start saying: My happiness is unlimited, and wonderful opportunities surround for me, and today nothing but the best is mine. Use your sense of humor, and you'll stop trying to change everything about yourself and learn to accept yourself. Stop taking yourself so seriously; lighten up mentally and you'll lighten up physically. Laughter is a great healer and has a physiological release mechanism for reducing stress.

GAME PLAYING: BE HONEST WITH YOURSELF

As of this moment, stop playing games with yourself, and be honest with yourself. When you play games with yourself you seldom win. Claiming you're buying cookies only for your family or you just can't pass up the two-for-one sale is creating the emotional weight that brings about physical weight. What about the drive home from the grocery store? Your hands are drawn to the cookies like magnets to a refrigerator, and pretty soon ... pff!—a whole role of cookies disappears. You panic because your family and friends know you are trying to control your eating problem and you search frantically for a way to get rid of the cookies, but feel you can't dare waste food by throwing it away. So the next best solution appears to be to simply finish the rest of the bag! After devouring the remainder of the bag, the same question surfaces, "What's wrong with me? I have no control." Here is where being honest with yourself can save you a lot of emotional and physical pain. You know that you are buying those cookies for you, and no one else. Be honest with yourself. If you are going to buy the cookies, bring them home and share them with everyone, or else don't buy them.

Get out of the artificial world of dieting. Eating off tiny plates so you think you're eating more is silly. Who are you really fooling? Chewing your food 200 times before swallowing, or drinking 15 glasses of water a day in hopes of losing weight, is a diet behavior. Fat and water don't mix. It is a fallacy to think that drinking water will help rid your body of fat. Water does help the kidneys and liver function more easily, and it is important for eliminating waste, transporting vitamins and minerals, and many other functions. Water is the most important nutrient in the body. Water can help control physical weight by taking the place of a sugary high-calorie drink and helping to fill you up—but it doesn't break down fat.

What's going to happen when you get back into the real world where eating means more than consuming carrots, lettuce, cottage cheese, and one-calorie diet soda? After eating like this for a week you then go to a party and vow not to eat anything—again you're playing a game, and you're not going to win. All week you were just avoiding food and not learning to control food, and at the party avoiding it is too difficult. Controlling your eating means controlling your mind, so create honest and realistic thoughts for yourself. If a person loses physical weight too quickly and doesn't understand how he did it, he will live in a state of panic, always being afraid of gaining weight. A young woman approached me after my lecture and said she had dreams about fat growing back on her thighs. As strange as this may seem, her tears showed how serious this was to her. She claimed to actually feel a tingling sensation in her thighs where she felt the fat accumulating. Take your time and understand the process so you don't always live in fear of gaining fat or feel guilt every time you eat!

This is why I dislike "before" and "after" pictures. A person may lose their physical weight, but emotional weight like fear and guilt and low self-esteem remains. Achieving a positive self-image and peace of mind is your ultimate purpose, and being honest with yourself is essential to achieving this. Peace of mind is an inside job and the place it exists is within you. Once you feel peace of mind, the mirror image will look more beautiful than ever.

BEVERLY

Beverly was in charge of grocery shopping for herself and her husband. She'd buy all kinds of "junk food" that was supposedly for her husband, but somehow her husband never got the chance to taste a morsel of these foods. Consciously, she bought these foods for her husband, but subconsciously, she was really buying them for herself. When I suggested that she wasn't being honest with herself and was buying these foods not for her husband but herself, she denied it, getting perturbed.

I then told her that if she wasn't buying these foods for herself, she should let her husband buy his own junk food. The next time she went shopping she told me it required a lot of control, and that she had noticed a big savings in her grocery bill and felt better about herself. Beverly saved not only money, but also her self-esteem, through being honest. She also told me that she was embarrassed once she realized her husband never even bought the junk food. They were *her* favorite foods. She brought this habit into awareness and then learned stimulus control through self-honesty. Beverly recalled our first session where she told me that since she got married she had been putting on weight. She now knows it was her own habits, not the marriage, that caused her physical and emotional weight.

PAM

Pam also learned stimulus control, and she learned how losing physical and emotional weight means being honest with herself. When Pam first visited me she was about 80 pounds overfat and had 200 pounds of emotional weight that she had painfully carried around with her for about 20 years. She admitted to having a weakness for sweets and knew the location of every bakery and candy shop in her town. Pam frequently made visits to bakeries, making sure she alternated going to each store so as not to be known as a "regular customer." When she did go into the bakery, she was too embarrassed to let anyone know she was buying for herself, so she would order a cake and request an inscription such as "Happy Birthday Alfred" so it would appear that it wasn't for her to eat. Even when Pam went to the grocery store, she would hide all the cakes, candy, and cookies she bought underneath the iceberg lettuce, carrot sticks, broccoli, and cauliflower. Pam referred to these foods as "rabbit food." She was not fooling anyone but herself, and she slowly realized she wasn't being honest with herself. One of Pam's first goals was to shop at only one bakery and to verbally say, "I want two jelly donuts." Just this goal alone resulted in Pam losing fat because she ordered much less than before. She lost 10 pounds of fat in four weeks and continued to eat limited amounts of sweets and chocolate on certain days. Pam applied honesty and stimulus control to her life. She began to trust herself around what she called "forbidden foods," and began to learn that chocolate and sweets had no power over her—it was only the power she gave them. Everyone can learn from Pam and her experience with setting small goals. These small goals led to significant changes in her body weight and her attitude toward herself.

Before, Pam would have set an unrealistic big goal and said, "I'm going to *stop* eating all sweets and chocolate." She would have become overwhelmed at the pressure she put on herself, and she would have quit. I have seen the same type of behavior in people who try to quit smoking by going "cold turkey." They go to such extremes because they are afraid of trusting themselves with cigarettes because they fear losing control. Pam started thinking more positively and started saying, "I can do it" and "I have control NOW!" The more Pam trusted herself, the more honest she was with herself, becoming happy, healthy and in control of eating.

Start by simply taking a grocery list with you. You will save yourself money and calories. Start eating before you go shopping. There is too much "food stimuli" in the grocery store to resist, and you will find it a lot easier to control your food purchases if you eat beforehand. Stimulus control also means cleaning out the cabinets and refrigerator of all foods you may binge on. If you don't have these foods around at first, you can slowly gain strength and control, eventually bringing these foods back into the house after you've learned to trust yourself.

For people who eat their meals out of vending machines, stimulus control means not bringing money with you to get a quick fix. Bring enough money for a phone call, and nothing else.

For a social function, eat a salad before going to events that have tempting foods. Talk and interact with people at the event. All these ideas are basic and to the point, for it is the basics in life that work.

LOOK WHAT YOU MADE ME DO!

Freedom comes with responsibility. Take responsibility for your actions, and controlling your eating will be easier. No one makes you eat anything—it is your choice. Take responsibility for yourself and become self-concerned—not self-centered and over-responsible for others' actions. Becoming overly responsible for others is a convenient way of avoiding dealing with your own life—always having to do for others because they "need you," and then never meeting your needs. No one makes you do anything. You're not a helpless victim of circumstance, for there is a permanent connection between what you are inside and what takes place in your life.

Taking responsibility for your actions also gives you a sense of control. You can no longer say "Look at what you made me do." It is "Look at what I did." Once you take full responsibility for your thoughts, feelings, and actions, you can be all alone in a room with your "binge foods" and still show control. You can make good choices for yourself, even when the disciplinarian (external motivator) isn't there. Let me explain further. When a person is on a "diet," almost everyone knows about it, don't they? Therefore, it is easier not to overeat when other people or the scale (external motivators) are around. Being alone, however, poses more of a challenge not to overeat. Choosing then not to overeat or select a healthier food is a positive indication that you have made a permanent, lifelong change in your behavior. Knowing whether you have made a permanent change requires you to ask yourself if, once you lose physical weight, you will continue to use what you have learned.

Another example of this idea can be illustrated using the example of a child's behavior. If Johnny is told by his parents to take out the garbage every day, and he does it only upon his parents' repeated requests, he has not made a permanent change in his behavior. Johnny's behavior was dependent on the disciplinarians (his parents) being there to make the request. Otherwise, the garbage wouldn't be taken out. Therefore, when behavior (good eating) continues independently of the disciplinarians (external motivators) it will become more of a behavior you are doing for yourself, making it a lifelong change.

VARIETY: A NECESSITY

Would you ever think of wearing the same clothes every day? If you did, it certainly would be *boring* and tiresome. Yet, when people want to lose fat they eat the same foods day after day, *boring* their taste buds to death and losing interest after a week.

Set yourself up for success! Apply variety to your thinking and to your eating. Don't bore yourself with carrot sticks. Keep your taste buds stimulated. Eating the same food all the time is the lazy and unsuccessful way to lose fat because it requires no organization or permanent change in one's lifestyle. A person just learns how to successfully *avoid* food—not *control* it.

ERIN

Erin decided to take my advice. At age 26, Erin had dieted all her life, and as a result had actually gained more weight through the years.

She said she was going to become food-wise this time! This was a good positive attitude, not like the other times she tried losing fat by dieting, which held so many negative feelings for her. Erin started eating a variety of foods and did a variety of different exercises, making her routine an interesting one. She worked hard at keeping her weight loss goals interesting. She realized that you can't just wait for things to happen, you have to make them happen—and that takes organization, and facing things you'd rather avoid. Erin's last statement to me was that variety was the spice of life and she lost her fat in a variety of ways. What she meant was that you don't lose physical weight by dieting; it happens because of a variety of things: *healthy eating, thinking, and exercise.*

MAKING POSITIVE ASSOCIATIONS

Your environment and the people you associate with are important to being happy and accomplishing your goals. Happiness will lead you to greater, more positive experiences in life. Happiness is a powerful emotion. It has special healing properties capable of keeping you in good health, while strengthening and prolonging your life. The next time you have a headache, stop before you reach for an aspirin and ask yourself, "How positive is my life and the people in it? Am I happy?"

Being in a positive, supportive environment with happy people will make your goals easier to achieve. If you have ever worked in an environment where people work closely together, you know that the negative attitude of one person can affect everyone. Prolonged association with negative people makes you negative and bitter. Negativity then becomes a habit (which, as we discussed earlier, is not always observable) and we can become deaf to our own negativity. Soon the negative person doesn't think they're being negative; they say they are "just being realistic." We can catch this negativity as easily as the common cold. The common cold has no cure, but negativity does.

Create then your own positive reality by positive thinking and positive associations with people. Fill your life with optimism. Start looking at the positive side of places, people, and conditions.

CHAPTER TWO: THINGS TO REMEMBER

* Stop being superhuman and be supersuccessful instead.

* You want to develop *control* over eating, not *over-control*.

* Be consistent, not perfect.

* Mistakes are really opportunities, helping you make better choices.

* Listen to yourself.

* Lighten up mentally and you'll lighten up physically.

* Focus more on the process and not so much on the end goal.
* Change negative habits to positive behaviors.
* Be honest with yourself.
* Get in tune with your natural body drives.
* There is never the perfect time, but the present is the right time.
* Peace of mind is an inside job, and the place it exists is within you.

ASK YOURSELF:

* What is my purpose?
* What would I tell a friend that has my same problem?
* If I would just be me, what would I be?
* Why do I want to change?

Say to yourself 3 times daily: "I'm healthy, happy, and in control of eating. I care about myself and am kind and compassionate." The only side effect is positive change!

3

Getting to the Root of the Problem

You wake up one beautiful morning and gaze out on your yard ... and discover to your chagrin that there are more weeds than flowers. You plan to get rid of the weeds that very day. Old floppy hat on your head, wearing unravelling cut-off jeans that show as much of you as they cover, you head out to do the task. What next? Do you daintily snip off the tops of the weeds, then merrily mince back into your house, thinking—hoping—that you have dealt with the problem, that those old nasty weeds are gone forever? No, of course not. Experienced gardener that you are, you know that you have to get down to the roots. You have to dig deep, taking the extra time and effort to get the whole plant gone. If you don't do so the weed will blossom again and again.

Much the same may be said of a weight problem. You wake up one morning, shuffle to the bathroom, step on the scale, and are jolted awake with a shock that a half dozen cups of coffee can't match. Your weight! Something has to be done about your weight! You could take a temporary measure—go on yet another diet. The results would be about as permanent as those you would get from snipping the heads off the dandelions and leaving the plants intact. To achieve permanent weight loss, you need to get to the root of the problem. Doing so may not be easy; it may even be frightening—but it *is* possible. Getting to the root of the problem means you must become aware of its existence, admit to it, and finally accept it. The "Three A's"—Awareness, Admittance, and Acceptance—are the steps to permanent weight control. Emotions are there to tell you whether your needs are being met. Emotions give you self-value.

AWARENESS:
WHEN THE GOING GETS TOUGH, WE STUFF

The first step is to become aware, especially when dealing with emotions. Emotions can be concealed in your subconscious mind and motivate you without your conscious awareness. Once you become aware of your emotions, your energy will flow more positively. You may act on your anger without realizing you are angry. You might feel anxious, fearful, or guilty on one day, and helpless, disappointed, or just unhappy the next. All of your emotions need to be brought into awareness so you can admit to them and accept them as being part of you. There are no negative emotions.

All emotions, even guilt, fear, and anger—when used in a positive way—can provide you with a better sense of who you are and where you want to go in life. Listen to your emotions—not just your conscious perceptions. Listen to yourself, don't just analyze yourself. When you say you're out of control of your eating, you are really out of control of your emotions. All emotions are valid, but sometimes you may not want to feel a certain way, so you ignore your emotions. Don't push your emotions away. Feel your emotions and work through them. Even happiness, or love if repressed can cause just as much emotional weight as anger, guilt etc.

Don't let the scale tell you how you are supposed to feel. Get in touch with your feelings. Don't look at the scale for approval—Trust yourself.

Your emotions—often involuntary responses—can't be turned off or gotten rid of, although you can control what you do about them. Don't say, "I shouldn't feel this way." Try not to get upset about feeling scared, insecure, guilty, or angry, but instead take responsibility for what you do with these emotions. You can learn to accept, trust, and control them, or you can push them away—but, don't ever turn them off. It is when you repress your emotions or push them away that they are no longer working in a positive way. Your emotions are then turned inward, motivating you without your conscious awareness, usually motivating you negatively. The more you repress or push away your true emotions, the more you'll turn to or away from food for comfort and control. This only serves as a temporary distraction, delaying getting to the root of the problem. Eating problems are in many cases emotions repressed. This can happen to even the healthiest person.

Eating is used not only for nutritional nourishment, but also for emotional nourishment. This is why you can eat and eat and never feel satisfied. You're eating not because of physical hunger, but because of emotional hunger. Eventually you'll begin to develop physical intimacies with food, instead of emotional intimacies with yourself, as eating becomes a more private event. Let's begin by becoming aware of your emotions, which means identifying the fact that you are sad, guilty, angry, disappointed, etc. Becoming aware of your emotions is just as important as what you are eating. You need to become emotionally aware, and not just focus on breakfast, lunch, and dinner.

Eating or not eating becomes your way of dealing with unwanted feelings or problems, moving you further from becoming aware of your true emotions, and eating becomes a sign of vulnerability. Your physical intimacies with food or the restriction of food become an obsessive-compulsive behavior, as do binging, purging and overexercising. So you must become aware of the reason behind eating or not eating, You may feel even now that something is wrong, but you don't know why. For now, the first step is to listen to your feelings and bring to mind new awareness, and not to worry about why! Just feel! Hurrying your emotions can't be done, any more than you can turn them off.

Begin statements with "I feel," which will help you become aware. Do you feel angry or disappointed because of the countless times you've had to start over, beginning each effort to overcome your eating problem feeling this way? Feeling this way and not being aware of it makes things more difficult to overcome, as your emotions build up and mix up, and the diet cycle begins—and you turn to or away from food for escape from these repressed emotions.

In life, anger, happiness, guilt, trust, disappointment, and love are all a part of living. Not being aware of your hidden frustration of always having to start over keeps you from trying to succeed. Deal with your emotions. Don't stuff them down with food or restrict food to punish yourself for feeling a certain way. When you do this, your psychological life becomes totally centered on eating or not eating, dieting, and exercising. If physical weight loss doesn't occur quickly enough, you then try harder to get thin and gain control, either by the further restriction of food, binging and purging, taking a few more laxatives, or exercising to exhaustion! These are all forms of self-punishment, as all your emotions boil within you. None of these self-punishing behaviors are the solutions; they only move you further from the real cause. It is easy to blame your failure or bad feelings about yourself on food or your body weight. You are not unhappy and confused because of your eating problem. It is your unhappiness and confusion that caused the eating problem. Physical weight is merely the symptom of emotions not dealt with. Most people tend to look toward the simpler, more pleasurable solution when wanting to change or solve a problem. It is easier and more pleasurable to eat or not eat than to face emotions or problems.

Thinking that your self-punishing behavior is a simpler, easier way to overcoming your eating problem is hurting you more on the inside and outside, and requires more effort and strength than it would to listen to your emotions and take responsibility for them. Remember, the refrigerator light isn't the light at the end of the tunnel, but it could be blinding you from seeing the real problem! The refrigerator doesn't say, "Close me!"

Hoping that perfect physical weight is synonymous with perfect life will only result in constant disappointment and self-deprivation of both physical nourishment (food) and emotional nourishment (feelings). Stop depriving yourself emotionally and physically, and start to take steps toward trusting yourself, discovering who you are through self-awareness. None of us enters a situation with an empty head or an absence of emotions. By *exploring* your emotions—not by repressing them or pushing them away—you can overcome your problem without such a terrible struggle.

The more you repress your emotions and try to feel or be something that you're not, the more you'll stay the same, continually turning to or away from food for comfort and control.

Your emotions are good. They are a part of you. Trust them and they won't let you down.

EMOTIONAL INTELLIGENCE

Your emotions and your intellect coexist within you. There is a unity, or link, between your cognitive intelligence and your emotional intelligence, because life is a thinking and feeling experience. I believe that how well you understand and direct your emotions is linked to how well you use your intellectual ability.

If emotions are not understood, they get in the way of our intellectual ability, and our ability to make decisions. The smartest person may allow their fear and anxiety to get in the way of their trying new experiences, like getting a better job or a new relationship. Your cognitive intelligence and emotional intelligence can clash when your emotions tell you, "I want to ... but I'm too old," or "I want to ... but I'm too fat or clumsy." Your repressed emotions will continue to surface until the message is understood and directed. When you push away or belitte the importance of your emotions, they begin to mix up. Fear—"I can't do it"—becomes anxiety—"I'll never make it." As you can see, as emotions mix up, the problems seem to become too difficult to solve. If you don't deal with your guilt it can lead to feelings of shame.

Listening to your emotions opens you to new experiences; this is the opposite of defensiveness. You can become more and more defensive as you ignore how you are feeling. These are ego defense mechanisms such as repression, denial, self-deprivation, and self-punishment. You use these defense mechanisms when something is seen as too threatening to express or experience. You may fear eating too much and losing control, so you punish yourself by not eating. You may fear rejection or criticism if you express your feelings, so you push them away and ignore them. Defense mechanisms are coping mechanisms that are needed for survival, but they can easily be overused, causing a painful and frustrated survival. These coping mechanisms are used when you feel your wishes or desires are incompatible with fulfillment. You then take these distressing thoughts and bar them from conscious expression, periodically turning to or away from food for comfort, control, and emotional support. The binging and purging are both coping mechanisms. Binging is a form of self-punishment, and purging is an emotional release. Also, another coping mechanism is food restriction, which is a form of denial. You are avoiding food instead of learning to trust yourself, which is a lot more threatening than not eating.

ELLEN

Ellen was too afraid to say what was on her mind and express how she was feeling. Instead she expressed herself in the best way she knew how—through an eating problem. Many times, when we repress our emotions, we are not aware of the motivation behind our behavior. We are simply trying to be happier and meet our needs in the best way we know how. Ellen used her eating problem as a way to communicate her emotional pain to others. Unaware of what she was doing, Ellen damaged her body through binging and purging. This physical damage she had done to her body now transformed her emotional pain that she could not express into a pain physically observable by others. Now her emotional pain was visible; it told people to take her seriously.

When I explained to Ellen how she was trying to express her emotions through her eating problem, she was shocked. For Ellen, the reason for her eating problem was unknown. Yet it had to stop, because even though it was a coping mechanism and a way of self-expression, it was also *self-destructive*.

Ellen was too frightened to give it up. She was binging and purging an average of four times daily, which was severe enough to require hospitalization. On the day of our third counseling session, Ellen was scheduled to be released. She was terrified by the thought of going home. I was happy to see Ellen was expressing her fear and trying to deal with it by talking, not just going home and resuming her binging and purging. We also discussed how she referred to herself as "nothing," or "being invisible," telling me that she was afraid once she left the hospital she might again become invisible.

I explained to Ellen that hospitalization had given her a way to express to people how she was hurting, and now I was going to help her learn to express her emotions in a much healthier way. I knew this thought was frightening to her, but I assured her I would be there to help. I hoped to provide Ellen with the same kind of security and assurance that she was getting from binging and purging, as well as being in the hospital, until she was strong enough to function on her own.

After several months of counseling, Ellen gained enough trust and confidence in me to begin expressing her emotions to me. Eventually she began expressing herself not only to me but also to her family and friends. Ellen no longer needs counseling, because she has become secure in expressing her emotions. Ellen also feels physically strong, because she keeps food in her body long enough for nutrients to be absorbed. Her exercise program, she claims, gives her immediate satisfaction, and helps her cope with stress.

For most of us food serves more of a purpose than just hunger. It can act as a distraction, moving us further away from dealing with our problems, while providing us with only a *temporary* means of coping. Even though food may temporarily reduce psychological stress for some people, it can at the same time also cause physical stress from the consumption of excess calories, leading to obesity, which is a risk factor for many diseases—including heart disease, high blood pressure, and diabetes.

ED

Ed noticed how food was serving as a temporary coping mechanism for him, and decided to change his ways. At age 43, Ed decided to relax and "clear his head." This was a completely new behavior for Ed, and this meant talking about his feelings—to me, to his family, and to his friends—which needless to say made him very uncomfortable. Ed had grown up with the idea that expressing feelings was really complaining, and "no one likes a complainer." He was also told—and believed—that expressing fears was not masculine, and would make others uncomfortable.

I felt it was essential that Ed learn to express his feelings because he had told me several times that others misunderstood him. I believed he needed to communicate better with people, and that this would naturally develop as he became more self-expressive. So that Ed did not feel too pressured about working toward his self-expression, I also emphasized the importance of nutrition, body metabolism, and developing daily exercise goals in reducing his stress as well as raising his fitness level. Ed soon became more sensitive to his emotions and learned to label his new way of communicating as self-expression, not complaining.

With much enthusiasm, Ed told me that people were understanding him more. I explained to him that becoming comfortable with his own emotions is central to everyone around him, and therefore helps him to become sensitive to their emotions as well, thereby increasing communication.

I had a chance to talk to Ed's wife, and she told me how much easier he was to live with knowing how he was feeling instead of living with his false silence. Ed is no longer the strong silent type, but has developed into the strong expressive type. Both Ed and his wife communicated how they were not just exchanging words when talking; now there was a real meeting of the minds.

In our closing session, Ed said how he actually enjoyed going to parties because he was no longer angry and resentful of others. He realized that he had to lose emotional weight first, before losing his 36 pounds of physical weight.

FRED

Fred, an attractive, intelligent, 28-year-old lab technician, arrived for his appointment obviously upset and hostile, as he slammed the door behind him. When I asked him what he was feeling, he rudely shouted, "Nothing! Why do you always ask me how I'm feeling? My feelings always get me in trouble! I'm too sensitive." Because I had grown used to Fred's outbursts, I immediately asked him how his day went, sensing that he had experienced distress in the last several hours. His first response was "Everybody's doing better than me; I'm nowhere! So tell me what's wrong with me—I'm paying you!" Fred had a tendency to compare himself with others, always coming up short as he became more and more self-critical and angry with himself. Yet his anger was usually directed at others because he wasn't dealing with the source of his anger. Fred's anger turned into hostility and self-destructive behavior, like overeating, as he tried to drown his anger in a six-pack of beer, adding to his feelings of worthlessness.

Fred finally sat down and relaxed. I told him that I could help him identify with his feelings, but it was up to him to change. During this session Fred set three goals that would help him feel better about himself and channel his anger in a positive direction to help himself. One source of Fred's anger was that he was extremely dissatisfied with his job and felt he was going nowhere. Fred's first goal was to write a new resume and bring it in the following week. The second goal was to begin an exercise program to feel better about his physical appearance, and the third goal was to make an effort not to compare himself to others. The following week Fred came to our session looking relaxed and more pleased with himself as he pulled a resume from underneath his arm and proudly held it out to me. Fred had also bought some new tennis shoes to use in his new exercise program. As for the third goal, Fred still compared himself to others, but also learned to accept not only *himself* as unique, but others as well. The new attitude gave him confidence to go after a higher-paying, more challenging job, which he achieved within three months

of our session. Fred lost 85 pounds of physical weight
and about 250 pounds of emotional weight.

JODI

Jodi, who had been married for 10 years, had been
feeling that her husband was not paying attention to her
needs for the last two years. When I asked her if she
had expressed her feelings to her husband, she angrily
replied, "Well, he should know—he's been married to
me for 10 years!" Jodi then began to explain what was
lacking in her relationship. Her well defined list ended
with feelings of guilt.

Even though she was angry with her husband, she
still felt guilty because she was not expressing these feelings. Jodi stated that trust and openness were greatly
valued in her relationship and that the guilt stemmed
from her own lack of openness and self-expression. Because Jodi's anger was not expressed, it was turned inward, creating feelings of guilt as she became resentful
and hostile. After several sessions, Jodi began to realize that she hadn't been expressing herself in other
areas of her life, such as with friends and family, but
had just been assuming that people would understand
her. I explained to her that people are not mind readers
and assumption can be very destructive to relationships.
Jodi soon learned that her problems had developed not
from others' inability to understand her, but from her
own lack of self-expression. This new insight caused her
to feel that she was in control of her life and had the
power to change things. Over the next seven months I
saw Jodi not only develop a healthier body through the
loss of 37 pounds of physical weight, but also develop
healthier relationships through her new sense of openness and self-expression. Jodi had now learned to develop emotional intimacies with others, instead of with
food.

Accepting and expressing emotions allows you to be understood better by others. Remember, people are not mind readers. They have difficulty helping when they don't understand your feelings.

Talk about your feelings with others. Have you ever been upset, trying to fight back tears, and yet when someone asks you "What's wrong?" you reply with, "Oh, nothing! Nothing's wrong!" Obviously, something is wrong. If nothing's wrong, why are you crying? Some part of you cares—maybe not your intellect, but your emotions. Identify how you're feeling. If you make a desperate attempt to get rid of your distress by binging on nachos and cheese dip, you still end up feeling no better—only worse—after binging. The feelings are still there!

You haven't gotten to the root of the problem. When you're saying, "Nothing's wrong," or "I don't care," you are still "feeling," but you are confining what you're feeling to your intellect, saying, "I don't care." Use your emotional intelligence and *start caring,* by becoming aware of what emotional needs you have that are not being fulfilled.

Here are some techniques, and some things to think about, that will help you become more aware of your emotions, putting to use your emotional intelligence:

* Begin statements with, "I feel ... "

* I feel happy when ...

* What would give you a peace of mind, and why?

* I get so angry when ...

* How does eating or not eating keep you safe?

* The guilt is overwhelming when ...

* Food makes me feel ...

* Why do I have the right to express my feelings?

ADMITTANCE: "THIS HURTS ME MORE THAN IT HURTS YOU"

Once you identify your emotions, which means you become aware they exist, you must admit to them as being real, not just imaginary. Admit to yourself that your emotions were meant to be expressed. Doing so helps you to further discover yourself, and allow others to discover you—the *real* you. You have the right to express your emotions. Admit to that right!

Admittance means you stop denying that you're angry, guilty, or sad. Your emotions are a vehicle for discovering yourself. As you start admitting to them, you naturally become more self-directed, relying on your own emotions. The more you admit to your emotions, the more you will begin to act in congruence with them, not feeling one way and acting another!—such as wanting to lose physical weight while you continue to overeat and don't exercise, or severely restricting food when you know it is not healthy. When you do something like this, your behavior is not in line with your attitude, creating negative feelings and a power struggle within you.

Putting and end to this struggle requires using emotional intelligence, so your emotions will be in congruence with your actions and you'll begin making positive changes. If you are angry, admit to your anger—it is telling you that you've been hurt, and that hasn't been expressed. Your feelings of guilt are telling you there's something you're not understanding. Your feeling of fear could mean you are avoiding something in your life; anxiety might be telling you there is something you're running from. When fear is not admitted, it can build up and mix up, and develop into feelings of anxiety, making change more difficult to face. Even though the problem hasn't changed, your built-up emotions have changed your perception of the problem; it seems more threatening. Admit to your emotions before they begin to build up and mix up—before emotional weight begins to form. As your emotions mix up, *you* mix up, as you make yourself anxious about being anxious, depressed about being depressed. By doing this you've made yourself feel guilty through self-condemnation—condemning yourself for feeling a certain way. Then you condemn yourself further for seeing that you condemned yourself and then didn't stop condemning yourself! Now *that's* mixed up! Eventually, it is difficult to remember the original problem, as more self-defeating, useless thoughts enter along with your self-condemning attitude, all of which represent more of the real problem.

Feeling bored is a good message if you listen to it and try to change this feeling by engaging in a new activity or new thought. Have you been dwelling on the same thought or problem for the last 15 years? If you need help in working out your feelings or problems, admit you need help and that it's *okay* to need people. If you're bored, change it. Admitting to a problem or emotion doesn't mean you just sit around for years admitting, while you think and think and think about your thinking, and then think about thinking about your thinking—think about it! A lot of people do this, saying, "Yes, I know there is a problem," and then never move toward the next step—*acceptance*.

JEFF

Jeff was about 60 pounds overfat and projected a stereotype of the jolly fat person. Outside, he always wore a smile while inside he was crying. He always had to be entertaining, joking, and making people laugh, while he himself remained depressed. As Jeff became more in touch with his emotions, he realized that he could only accept himself if others thought well of him. He needed outward approval from others because he wasn't getting it from himself! In counseling, Jeff became aware that he didn't have to *sell* himself, he just had to *be* himself, realizing that you don't have to sell a good thing. After a few weeks, Jeff started bringing into session such insights as "It's not what other people think I am, but what *I* think I am."

I have seen this attitude in many of my clients. I refer to this as *mechanical* observations from others about themselves instead of *emotional* observations from within. Mechanical observations are usually fulfilling others' expectations of you, while you're never fulfilling your own expectations. You're always doing well by others but not by yourself. If this is you, you have become a *people pleaser*. What Jeff was feeling was his own power struggle, an ego defense mechanism called *reaction formation*. This is when an individual replaces an anxiety-eliciting impulse, like Jeff's low self-esteem, with behavior that is the exact opposite, being jolly and happy. You probably know an individual (could it be you?) who replaces an anxiety-eliciting impulse (like dieting) with behavior that is the exact opposite (overeating). There is a power struggle between wanting to be thin and not wanting it, or wanting to express emotions but being afraid of criticism. Many times your emotions are in conflict with how you *want* to feel. Like Jeff, you may be angry or sad inside and happy outside. You are storing up your emotions until they finally burst into a night of uncontrolled compulsive overeating. This is sometimes referred to as a passive-agressive personality, which can be frustrating because you are never feeling or doing what you want.

Dieting and exercise alone can't address all the reasons behind eating or not eating, yet this is what people primarily focus on—forgetting all about the mind!

The outside symbols are the "mechanics" of weight control. They tell you the appropriate "normal" steps to follow. First you join an aerobics program, then you stay away from all the "forbidden" foods that are supposedly the cause of all your problems, and lastly, stay close to the scale. However, the more you avoid foods, the more you learn not to trust yourself. If you do eat those "forbidden" foods it only reinforces your distrust in yourself. Just because the anorexic starts eating, the bulimic stops binging, or the overweight person loses weight doesn't mean the underlying problem is solved. This merely *symptom removal*. It is all about developing a positive self-image and peace of mind!

MARCY

Marcy, an 18-year-old, was extremely unhealthy and severely thin. Marcy admitted she was afraid of getting fat and felt that food had a power over her. She was diagnosed by her doctor as anorexic. As our sessions progressed, Marcy realized that she was not afraid of getting fat, but of trusting herself. Through self-exploration, Marcy found that the underlying reason for her unwillingness to trust herself was that she had a tendency to do too much too soon and over-obligate herself. Marcy's constant over-obligation was actually her attempt to feel good about herself, yet it continued to backfire.

In other words, Marcy's intentions were good, just misdirected. Her over-obligation led to feelings of being overwhelmed due to the pressure she put on herself. Marcy began to set realistic goals within a comfortable time frame, one that would give her at least a chance to succeed. In our next session Marcy had a long list of obligations. As she ran over the list, she stopped and laughed at herself, realizing that she had once again over-obligated herself. This was great progress because she admitted her problem and began restructuring her goals. Marcy's renewed confidence and self-control helped her to view food for what it is—physical nourishment, not emotional nourishment.

JACKIE

Jackie walked into the office and promptly informed me that six doctors had diagnosed her as being bulimic/anorexic and that the only reason she came to me was to avoid hospitalization. Jackie was 16 years old, and 5 feet 4 inches tall. She had dropped from 143 pounds to 80 pounds in the last two months and was extremely proud of this. She told me, "I like the way I look and don't want to change." Jackie was the perfect example of the distorted self-image—she saw herself as fat, when in reality, she was grossly underweight. Jackie played it tough and in control externally, but she was just too afraid to admit her emotions—especially with regard to trusting others. She looked pale and malnourished, her hair was thinning, and she appeared anxious and distressed.

Jackie was very smug about her new-found bulimia. "Now," she said, "I can eat without getting fat and don't have my stupid period." She was no longer a starving anorexic but a bulimic/anorexic. Jackie felt she had the answers to everything and that no one understood or cared about her, so she had built walls around herself by playing it tough. She had a poor relationship with her parents and manipulated them through crying, screaming, and constant threats of further weight loss. Her technique worked—they were terrified of her.

Jackie thought she could manipulate me the same way, and tried to use her need to be thinner and her crying as a distraction to avoid getting to the root of the problem. For the first six sessions she tried to test me (to see how strong I was) by doing such things as drinking 8-10 glasses of water before coming to the session to show an increase on the scale, but much to her surprise there *was* no scale. While it would have been easy to think of Jackie as a "brat," what she really needed was to reach out and trust someone by learning to express her emotions. It wasn't until she began trusting me that she allowed herself to be vulnerable and realized I wasn't threatened by her behavior as her parents were.

As I got to know Jackie, I saw she had a real problem with trusting anyone, and she didn't have any friends as a result. She isolated herself from people, thinking of others as "stupid" and "weak." Before she could trust me she wanted to make sure I was strong enough to handle her threats. I came to realize that Jackie used her life-threatening behaviors— anorexia and bulimia—as a defense mechanism to repel others, making sure no one could get close enough to her to hurt her. She would never have to trust anyone, or open herself up to vulnerability.

It was still difficult for Jackie to start eating food because her defense mechanism worked so well for her. Jackie was another example of *emotional weight*. She thought she was too heavy at 123 pounds, when actually her dissatisfaction with herself was due not to her weight but tho her inability to trust herself or others. Jackie's heaviness lay in her own mind. She had to *admit* emotions in order to get to the root of her problem. Slowly she began to gain weight. I made sure she was comfortable with her weight as she learned to open up and trust others.

TECHNIQUES FOR ADMITTING YOUR EMOTIONS

Here are some exercises that will help you admit to your emotions, bringing you another step closer to fulfilling your needs instead of turning to or away from food for fulfillment.

* Expressing my emotions is important because...
* I feel angry when...
* I feel anxious about...

* I'm happiest when...
* I sometimes feel _____ but act like _____
* The power struggle within me is...
* I admit that my emotions are important to express, so they no longer continue to mix up and build up.

ACCEPTANCE: ACKNOWLEDGING THE POWER OF FOOD

We all wish food were powerful enough that it could wipe out problems and totally improve our lives. But food has no power except the power we give it, and using food for emotional support or fulfillment gives it power. Labeling food good or bad also gives it power. Using food this way can be stopped once you accept that it is *okay* to be angry, sad, guilty, or even happy. Some people feel uncomfortable with being happy, and can't accept deserving to be happy. Acceptance means taking responsibility for what you do with your emotions. If you're hurt, express it; if it is a fear, take steps toward facing it. Put your fears in front of you so you'll stop looking back to see if they're still there.

Acceptance requires acting on your problem by taking visible steps toward change! Accepting the problem means you confront it and do something about it. If your boat stalled in the middle of the lake and you had two perfectly good paddles, would you just sit there? You might sit there just for a moment, become aware of what is around you, admit you have a BIG problem, and then accept that you're going to have to row in, realizing the easy way out would be to wait for someone to help, but that's not likely to happen. Are you looking for the easy way out even though you are perfectly capable of getting out of your situation? Don't just sit there in your boat, because it isn't going anywhere—start rowing! You are now past the admitting stage of

"I need to or will eat healthier" and are on your way to "I am eating healthier."

Take the action needed to get out of a situation that is causing you unhappiness, and if you need help, accept responsibility to reach out now and get help. We all need each other. No one is any better or worse; we are just at different levels in life.

Don't turn to or away from food for emotional support. Instead get to the root of the problem. If you are feeling depressed, don't say "I shouldn't feel this way," and begin to mix up your emotions, becoming more depressed about being depressed, or beginning to worry about worrying! In many cases feeling depressed is a time in which you can slow down and take a look at yourself and your life and become introspective. It can be a time where you become familiar with yourself again. A lot of people are uncomfortable with feeling depressed because they fight the feeling and don't accept it by experiencing it and working through it! When you're driving in your car and you pass a beautiful sight you slow down or you can't see it. Being depressed slows you down so you can take a look at yourself.

Accepting your emotions also means redirecting your energies. It takes a great deal of creative planning, organization, strength, and effort to conceal many of your self-destructive thoughts and actions. There is even a little gratification and power felt when you successfully restrict food, because you are seen as strong where most people aren't. Unfortunately this is short-lived and quickly becomes less and less rewarding as you experience physical and psychological pain. I recall in one of my lectures an obese man entering, looking bored and irritated. During the lecture he seemed restless and eager to leave, as he kept glancing at the door. When I asked for questions, he raised his hand quickly and he said, "I don't like what you're saying, but you're right!" He continued, "It's easier for me to blame my weight for all my problems. I know for sure

I can control my weight, but I'm not sure I can control my problems." This man had admitted that he had a problem. Many people in the audience also admitted to using food as a protective device or a drug to distract themselves, momentarily numbing themselves from their painful present existence. We can form many distractions by diverting our feelings, only to have them quickly return to our awareness after the distraction has subsided. For instance, when you are devouring mounds of fudge ripple ice cream swimming in gobs of chocolate syrup, surrounded by nuts, heaped with fresh whipping cream, and topped with a cherry for a finishing touch, little is entering your mind other than the pleasant sensation of eating. All mental and physical energies are centered on eating and your thoughts are far removed from present problems. While you are eating, you feel a sense of relief, but your problems are still there. Food is just acting as a temporary emotional support for the problems you are not admitting and accepting.

The more you repress your emotions and refuse to practice the Three A's (awareness, admittance, and acceptance), the more you find yourself eating in *negative mood states*. You then feel *out of control* of your actions, as eating becomes a mechanical, feelingless experience. Actually, it's your *emotions* that are out of control, as expressed through overeating, food restriction, binging, or purging.

When you eat in a negative mood state you may feel you have eaten a lot, even though you've eaten very little. The heaviness lies more in your mind than in your body—*emotional weight*. Actually, it is your emotions that are out of control, as expressed through eating. Now you may be thinking, "I eat when I'm happy, too." Being happy is still a part of your emotions that you may need to learn to express without the use of food. Think about this! Sometimes when you're happy you might say, "Oh, who cares," just like you do when you're feeling negative about yourself.

All eating problems share common features. Many people say they feel trapped in their bodies, but they are really trapped within their own emotions, wanting to express them but being too afraid.

Your body is just one part of you. Your mind is why you can lose weight and still feel heavy, seeing yourself as fat, or why a thin person can hate his or her body just as much as a fat person. About 95% of people—women *and men*—who lose weight will gain it back in one year or less because they haven't overcome their eating problem, but just learned to avoid food. These people haven't made mind and body changes. Their mental changes haven't met up with their physical changes.

Even though food may seem to be the central problem, it is not. The person who binges and purges does not always eat huge quantities of food. They may have something as healthy as a tuna sandwich, an apple, and a glass of milk, and feel this is too much food to eat. It wouldn't have mattered if this person ate three cherry pies, a gallon of ice cream, or a small salad and then purged. The motive behind consuming a small or large amount of food is the same. It is an emotional hunger, not just a physical hunger. Both men and women with eating problems have learned to displace their fears, disappointments, low self-esteem, and unhappiness onto food. Eating or not eating keeps them in control, safe, and secure. Overeating is a way to cope through the use of food, while emotions are ignored.

Emotions such as fear, love, happiness, guilt, disappointment, anger, low self-esteem, and self-doubt cannot be weighed in pounds and are not stored in your fat tissue. Losing fat doesn't mean you'll lose these feelings. You must accept those feelings as a first step: *find the feelings, and lose emotional and physical weight ... permanently!*

CAROL

This idea was difficult for Carol, age 19, to accept, as she insisted that food was her problem. Carol had been to four other eating disorder counselors before me. Initially Carol came to me because she wanted to eat less. She was already eating very little food, yet she viewed herself as a compulsive overeater. Because Carol had labeled herself a compulsive overeater, she was reacting to that label. Remember, the way we label ourselves in our life is the way we will react—and the label sticks.

In our next session Carol painfully told me she had been binging and purging for about eight months. We then began to discuss how food was not her problem. But she was much more certain that she could control the food she placed in her mouth than she was about her ability to control her problems and emotions. I then explained to her that her insistence on the idea that she binged because she ate too much food was an unconscious rationalization (coping mechanism), when in actuality she was eating very little.

Yet, if she admitted that she was eating only a little food, it would mean that her purging was not the result of food, but the result of a much deeper problem. Again, food was something she knew she could control. Her problems were not.

It took time for Carol to accept this idea. I had to help her face her problems and repressed emotions by providing her with the same security and emotional support that she was getting from her eating problem. I did this by letting her know that she didn't have to be alone with her fears and that I was there for her. I also tailor-made an eating plan for Carol, teaching her about the four basic food groups and basic nutrients.

Within a few months Carol started to deal with her emotions and problems, getting to the root of why she had an eating problem. Whenever Carol felt an urge to binge and purge again, she now knew that it was a signal telling her that there was a problem to solve or emotions to be expressed.

I was glad Carol came to see me because she was on the verge of becoming an anorexic. Dealing with anorexia is difficult because the fear of becoming obese does not diminish as weight loss progresses. However, the fear is carried with them even when they are dangerously thin. I have counseled anorexics that have lost weight so quickly that skin begins to hang because the body has been reduced beyond the skin's ability to shrink. The anorexic then begins to think that the soggy skin is fat, which then reinforces the further restriction of food. This is why it is important to seek help as soon as possible. A person with an eating problem begins to take more and more life-threatening means the longer the problem prevails.

If you think you or someone you know has an eating problem, get help as fast as possible. Don't wait! Remember, it's okay to need people and receive help. You don't have to be alone with your fears.

CONNIE

Connie, a 27-year-old high school English teacher, had been referred to me by her physician, who thought that she had not quite solved her problems and needed more assistance. Connie had recently been hospitalized. Her frequent vomiting damaged her esophageal walls, triggering a rupture, resulting in hemorrhage. Due to Connie's frequent vomiting, her teeth were bathed in hydrochloric acid from her stomach, causing enamel breakdown and severe decay.

Connie confessed that she was still binging and purging, but was down to three times a week instead of seven. She told me she was not completely over the break-up of her three-year relationship with her boyfriend, who still occasionally visited her. Connie also said she was aware that she was still hanging onto her old boyfriend because of her low self-esteem.

Because Connie wasn't feeling good about herself she had stopped socializing and spent most of her time alone with food, binging and purging. She felt that food wasn't going to hurt her, but developing another relationship might. Connie had to get out of her rut and take a risk if she wanted to change. Taking a risk meant she had to express her feelings and trust herself.

I began seeing her twice a week instead of just once to give her extra support. We started having lunch together in the office to allow Connie to become more comfortable with eating. The first time we had lunch, Connie regurgitated most of her food, because it was still too threatening and fearful to her. She was afraid to trust herself around food in fear of losing her false sense of control. As we had more lunches together, she began to trust me and slowly became more comfortable with trusting herself. I constantly reinforced the idea that she would not get fat from eating but would develop a healthy, lean body weight and once again be emotionally and physically strong.

Within the first month and a half of healthy eating, Connie regained her menstrual cycle, which had stopped three years previously. She also gained back 15 pounds of lean body mass, which made her feel like she was functioning more normally. Connie was the first client I had who stopped binging from the very first day she joined. She also worked hard toward improving her self-esteem and even switched careers to one more satisfying to her. Connie began socializing with men other than her ex-boyfriend.

Connie began a daily exercise program which she enjoyed so much that she even became a part-time aerobics instructor. Instead of trying to control her weight and life through binging and purging, Connie found a healthier way through exercise and positive thinking.

VANESSA

Vanessa, age 41, had a great many emotions she had been repressing for years. She lost a part of her identity about 10 years ago and was now actively searching for herself again, finding it an arduous and painful experience. Every time Vanessa was happy, she would say to me, "Things are just going too well. Something has to go wrong." It wasn't until she stopped fighting her emotions that she started to accept that she deserved to be happy and weight loss occurred. It was obvious that Vanessa was afraid to be happy, afraid that something terrible would follow her happiness; therefore she would frequently sabotage her success by overeating just to prove things weren't going that well! Soon she accepted deserving to be happy and became so.

You'll never get what you don't think you can have or deserve. Vanessa is no longer overweight or afraid to be happy. Being aware of, admitting, and accepting your emotions, like Vanessa, means you can take control over your actions—you no longer feel you are being motivated by some unknown force, but by yourself! You're in control. Food has no power or control over you! It does not call you from another room; it only has what power you decide to give it. And using it for emotional support is giving food a great deal of power.

KRISTIN

I received a call one day from a very concerned mother telling me of her 20-year-old daughter, Kristin, who wasn't eating much and was losing weight at an accelerated speed. She recently had moved back home after deciding to quit college. Kristin came to my office with her parents, but was very despondent and let her parents do most of the talking. When I asked her how she felt about what her parents were saying, she said, "I guess so." When I asked her why she wasn't eating, she said she wasn't hungry, why didn't everyone just leave her alone. I asked her if she felt good about herself and was happy with the way she looked. Again

she responded with "I guess so." Kristin knew her silence made others uncomfortable, and she watched her
parents squirm every time she said, "I guess so." I told
her I would see her only if she wanted to, not just if her
parents wanted her to.

As I began to see Kristin alone she opened up and
expressed how she felt that her parents dictated her
life. Her anorexia was her own silent way of getting
back at her parents; it was something she thought she
could control, and they couldn't do anything about it.
She was torn emotionally and was very angry, using her
anorexia to punish her parents and then feeling guilty
about her anger toward them. When I asked her if she
ever talked to her parents she said she didn't want to
hurt them.

Kristin felt that her love from her parents was very
conditional, based on her accomplishments. After several months, she began to understand her parents better
and express herself better to them. Once Kristin started
setting goals for what she wanted in her life, instead of
what she thought her parents wanted, she was a much
happier person and started using food for physical nourishment. It was her own expectations that caused her
pain and confusion. She was also able to give up her
obsessive behavior with food, no longer restricting herself to 500 calories a day. She began to eat a variety
of foods and started eating out at restaurants. Kristin
became slowly able to trust herself and feel confident
in expressing her emotions. She realized that when she
pushed away her feelings she gave food its power.

EXPRESS YOURSELF

You may be thinking right now, "Oh sure, that's
easy for her to say. The ideas of awareness, admittance,
and acceptance are easier said than done. I'll never be
able to practice what she is preaching." You're right ...

and wrong. It is easier said than done, but you will be able to practice what you have learned.

The scale is no longer your best friend. Your emotions and the expression of your emotions are, along with your Kleenex box! Remember, you're not alone. No matter what you're going through, someone else has gone through it, or something quite similar to it, before.

You don't have to be alone with your fears. By believing you're alone you'll feel more ashamed and hide or deny your feelings and your eating problem, pretending everything is fine when it is not! Asking for help doesn't mean you're helpless or less independent—it shows confidence, and strength. Asking for help is the first step to expressing your emotions.

Perhaps reading a few more case studies of people who have had—and worked through—problems of their own by getting to the root of the problem will be helpful.

GRACE

At age 32, Grace had been successfully establishing herself in a prestigious law firm, with strong hopes of eventually becoming a partner. Grace tended to view life in a black-and-white framework, very seldom allowing her emotions to direct her. This black-and-white, rigid way of thinking never allowed her to experience unconditional acceptance of herself or her feelings. Her love for herself was based on condition after condition. She was either good or bad, happy or sad, successful or unsuccessful. Up to this point in her life, all of her major decisions had been made with her calculating logic, and she was surprised to hear of something called emotional intelligence.

Her well developed intellect was not of any use to her in dealing with her emotions. Unable to identify with her emotions intellectually, she pushed them away, repressed them, and then placed another condition on herself, setting off a chain reaction: becoming depressed, she made herself depressed about being depressed. Her repressed emotions manifested themselves in constant feelings of anxiety, prompting further feelings of worthlessness. Since Grace's intellect had been getting in the way of her emotions, she felt her feelings of depression were related to a weight problem, which was why she came to see me. I was able to determine that Grace did not have a problem with anorexia or bulimia, since her strong intellect told her they were unhealthy behaviors, yet her basic eating habits did require improvement. Tears began to build in Grace's eyes and I asked her what she was feeling. She responded with, "I don't know—I just don't know." I tried to calm Grace by telling her to take a few deep breaths and relax, and to stay with her feelings. From this point on I asked Grace to tell me how she was feeling, rather than what she was thinking. I had her begin her sentences with "I feel," instead of "I think." Slowly, Grace began to get more in touch with her feelings and started liking herself. For the first time in her life she discovered a whole new part of herself that had been left behind.

As she became more accepting of her emotions, she began to trust them more, thus feeling more stable and more in control. She realized that her emotions and intellect should coexist in order to achieve a healthier mind. Grace didn't have to lose a pound physically, but she lost several pounds of unexpressed emotions. It was *emotional weight*. Grace was with me five months, and at her last session she expressed how she had felt she was leaving with not only a healthy body but a healthy mind.

THE HELPLESS VICTIM

Steve, a 43-year-old insurance salesman, about 6 feet 4 inches with broad shoulders, stood as he looked around the office and appeared very curious as he paged through several psychology books on the shelf. I asked him to sit on the "hot seat," a nickname I'd given to the chair most of my clients sit in during counseling. He quickly replied, "Do I have a choice?" I told him that we all have choices in life and if he would like to sit on the floor or stand he was more than welcome. This was one of the many tests Steve tried to impose on me during our sessions, indirectly challenging me. When I asked Steve to tell me a little bit about himself, he said, "Well, there's not much to say. I lost my business about 10 years ago." When I asked him how he felt about it, he responded with, "Well, that's life. I replied with, "Well, what's life?" He then complained that things just happen and there's nothing you can do about them. I asked him how he dealt with such a negative attitude and, as he patted his huge stomach, he said, "Well, can't you tell? I eat!" His laughter after this comment showed Steve's good sense of humor. Steve had already attended one of my lectures and he told me he came to see me because he liked my philosophies, and recalled my saying that many times our weight is not the cause of our problems, but our problems the cause of our weight. I then asked Steve if he thought he was a helpless victim in life. He replied, rather sarcastically, "Well, it's much easier that way." Steve eventually realized that this was his way of dealing with his anger, rather than redirecting it in a positive way. As Steve's emotions were building, so was the width of his body. I told him if he continued to repress his anger, he was headed for an emotional and/or physical disaster. I asked Steve what he thought his purpose in life was. One of my philosophies is that a lack of self-purpose in life leads many into a feeling of helplessness: the helpless victim in life with no purpose. We continued to define more specifically Steve's needs, wants, and desires, working toward making each a reality. Steve discarded his helpless victim attitude by admitting and accepting that he was angry. He started participating once again in his life. He began planning for the future, not only planning for breakfast, lunch, and dinner. He now felt he was important enough to take care of his health, and he began eliminating his frequent bouts with sugar; weight loss followed. Steve felt he gained back the time he had lost and was determined to add not only years to his life but life to his years.

THE CHRONIC DIETER

Lisa, a 31-year-old housewife, told me she had "let herself go" and had started putting on weight after her first child. She now had three children and said she was finding it increasingly difficult to lose her 40 pounds of excess fat. She expressed how she had tried every diet in existence (her most recent attempt was the "Last Chance Diet") and questioned her ability to succeed at weight control after failing even at the Last Chance Diet. She said she was feeling quite hopeless and didn't really know if I could help her. She even brought the results of her last physical to prove that she was in good health and was now searching for a deep psychological reason behind her inability to lose weight. During the past several years, Lisa's life had centered around her husband and children and meeting their needs, while ignoring her own. Coming to see me was an important step for Lisa because she was finally doing something completely for herself, yet she still felt extremely guilty because she could have bought her children new shoes instead of spending money on herself. Lisa was determined to do something for herself and was quite enthusiastic. Of course, like everyone else, she wanted to lose as much physical weight as possible within one week. I explained to her that I didn't believe in quick weight loss. Within the first week, Lisa became discouraged with only a one-pound loss and began to settle back into her old habits of giving solely to her family, ignoring herself. Using the scale only discouraged Lisa and hindered her motivation. We discussed the connection between her family and her avoidance behavior, and Lisa became very angry. I then told her I was sure that she loved and cared for her family very deeply, but again was using them as an avoidance behavior, not getting to the root of her problem. We then discussed how liking herself better would in turn help her to be a better mother and wife, taking responsibility for her own life, no longer blaming others for her inability to fulfill her own needs. This meant she couldn't give up easily on herself because she could no longer use her family as an excuse. Lisa started to lose emotional and physical weight because she was now looking at not only how she was eating, but how she was feeling as well. Lisa began to pay attention to her own needs, no longer gorging herself as she watched "As the World Turns."

Instead, she treated herself to tennis lessons, taking responsibility for her own happiness.

THE ATTENTION GETTER

Karen, a fashionably dressed 21-year-old, walked into my office one day looking quite terrified. She told me that she had just lost 20 pounds and was very afraid that she would regain it. I sensed in her desperate voice that there was something she wasn't telling me, and I questioned her about it. She began to cry and pulled a box of laxatives from her purse and admitted that she had used them both to lose weight and to keep it off, coupled with binging and purging. She told me that the laxatives were becoming a big expense, and she had searched all over town for the cheapest brands. After I explained to her the biological effects and potential dangers, she was very eager to change her self-destructive behaviors. As I began to counsel Karen, I found that her use of laxatives, as well as binging and purging, went a lot deeper than just weight control. As I got to know Karen better, I learned that she had been using these destructive methods as a way to regain her boyfriend's affections. Her boyfriend became quite concerned about her and smothered her with the attention she so desperately craved. As much as she wanted to stop these destructive behaviors, she feared once again the possibility of losing the love and care of her boyfriend. Karen had been in and out of hospitals for five years and was afraid of losing the security of the doctors and the hospitals if she recovered. Recovery meant letting go of not just what seemed to be her eating problem, but all of her security. If she recovered, who would pick up the pieces if she later failed? After six months of counseling Karen discovered her own uniqueness through awareness, admittance, and acceptance of her emotions. She realized she had the ability to pick herself up, and no longer needed to maintain her body weight or her relationship with her eating problem.

Karen expressed her fears and worked through them, sometimes experiencing pain, but positive results always followed. This gave her the security within herself she needed to continue on, forming healthy dependencies, not needy ones!

She began to exercise and eat nutritiously, not obsessively. As Karen's self-worth improved she began to say, "Laxatives, binging, and purging are history. It's history, honey!"

ACCEPTING EMOTIONS

Here are some techniques that will help you accept your emotions, which means accepting responsibility for them:

* Practice expressing your emotions.

* Get help or guidance—it is okay to need people.

* Expressing emotions means that saying NO is your freedom of choice.

* Become aware that many of your so-called hungers are emotional, not physical.

* Accept that food is just part of the problem. Once you express your emotions you'll no longer turn to or away from food for comfort and emotional support.

* Form healthy dependencies, not needy ones.

ONE OF THE MOST IMPORTANT THINGS TO REMEMBER:

Try and be consistent not perfect. Inconsistency is an Emotional Abuse, which can cause you to become so discouraged that you completely push your emotions away. Even the person who has a long-term eating problem can and does recover. Each person must search to discover their individual causes and needs, and bring to action the Three A's: awareness, admittance, and acceptance, as part of the search to recovery, while giving themselves the time they need to succeed.

4

Give Yourself Time to Succeed

I would presume that you are a busy person, and being busy is seen as an attractive personality attribute. It usually indicates you're ambitious, bright, and outgoing. Yet, it can get out of hand when suddenly you are no longer controlling time, and time is controlling you. Time may really be on your side, but only once you learn to use it. There is much truth in the phrase, "Time flies when you are having fun." What about how slow it can go when you're at the office and things aren't going well?

Time has nothing to do with it; it was how you were experiencing time. Time didn't speed up or slow down. When trying to overcome your eating problem, giving yourself time to succeed is crucial. Allow yourself time just in case you make a mistake and need to reorganize your efforts. So many creative and good thoughts never materialize because you didn't allow enough time. It's not because you are stupid or lack potential, or that it wasn't a good idea. You just didn't give it time to grow.

The next time you want to try and overcome your eating problem but feel your effort doesn't produce results quickly enough, go to the store, buy some seeds, and plant them. If your plant doesn't grow fast enough will you just rip it out of the ground? Or would you care for it, and supply it with a little more sunshine and water, giving it a chance to grow? You probably give many other experiences in your life time to grow. Why not give yourself equal time to bloom as you would give your plant? When you feel yourself growing impatient, start to care more for yourself!

Permanent changes take more time because they evolve from within. It is similar to painting a room a different color. Some people may clean the walls before painting. This takes more time, yet prevents the paint from chipping, resulting in a more permanent paint job. Not washing the wall takes less time, but may not be as permanent.

I recall reading what Thomas Edison once said: "The greatest human weakness lies in giving up too soon." Positive change demands strength, determination, mistakes, disappointments, and a positive, flexible mind that can adjust to taking a new direction. Possessing these qualities and working through the disappointments and mistakes ensures that once you change, you'll say, "I deserve to be here, and I feel comfortable." Quick changes leave people with a feeling of being lost and undeserving and uncomfortable with the change. To make a permanent change you must feel as though you deserve it. Giving yourself time to succeed helps you create this deserving feeling and permanently overcome your eating problem.

CATCH-22

Pushing and forcing your way though life ensures one thing only—burnout. Why then, do you continue this pushing and hurrying yourself to reach a goal? This whole process of quick results and fast and efficient thinking is great if you own a hamburger stand and want a quicker way to make more hamburgers.

When you're trying to making important personal changes in your life, pushing and hurrying is a Catch-22. These changes cannot be forced or hurried. This happens because you are uncomfortable with your body weight and naturally want to change it as soon as possible, to rid yourself of these bad feelings. So you buckle down, put your nose to the grindstone, take a deep breath, and start to force and hurry a process that can't be hurried—if permanent change is one of your goals.

Eventually, you burn out and get too tired to even think about making a positive change, feeling like you just don't care. Using fad diets, pills, diet patches, creams, and special fat-burning diet drinks, is a Catch-22. Using these gimmicks time and time again with no positive change wears you out. You get tired, and them someone like me comes along as says, "You can do it, by eating healthy, thinking healthy, and using your own potential."

But, by this point you're too burned out to listen to someone who wants you to use your energy and potential—you're too tired! Again, you begin to choose what you think is a quicker, easier way that doesn't require so much effort. Little do you know, the gimmick is what is tiring you out, as you have to continually deal with starting over and feeling like a failure. It is a Catch-22, and the creators of these products know this, and count on you returning several times to use their product. As they smile, you frown, while you drain your pocket of another $15 and your self-esteem of a little more pride. What gives these gimmicks so much success is your tiredness and disillusionment with yourself. The more tired you become, the more you search for a quick solution. Being tired can almost make you feel crazy, because the littlest decision, like what to have for dinner, becomes a major source of frustration.

The more you hurry and push yourself, the more you also push away your emotions, like the anger of having to control your eating again, or the built-up guilt for all those times you tried, but didn't make it, and haven't forgiven yourself. Coupled then with the fear that it may not work again, this boils inside you. These emotions eventually boil over and your goal quickly ends, and your emotions go down to a simmer.

Deal with these simmering emotions before they boil over. Take the time out to work on forgiving yourself, not starving yourself. Your experiences in life, good or bad, can be a means of making you become more aware of what you are doing now. Nothing is a waste of time if you grow and learn from it. Accept your experiences up to now and extract every bit of good from them. You can never forget them, but you can forgive yourself and go on! It is over. Let it go!

Write down some of the things you are carrying on your shoulders and forgive yourself or someone else. Sometimes understanding something and why it happened requires moving on in life. Move on by giving yourself time to succeed, and slow down and get rid of your emotional weight. Here are a few exercises that will help you break your Catch-22.

Slow down and relax. Then take a goal and visualize over and over again the steps you'd take to accomplish it. Use positive visualization to create steps on how you will gain control and overcome the obstacles as you clearly see your goal as obtainable and successful. Always take nice deep breaths, breathing in happiness, not short, quick, shallow breaths. You may be releasing too much carbon dioxide and be hyperventilating.

Before you do this exercise, think to yourself some good positive thoughts:

* My experiences in life will be good; I deserve the best and will receive it now.

* Right now, forgiveness and healing take place in my life; my happiness and ability to understand myself are not limited.

* Right now, wonderful opportunities surround me.

* I believe, right now, I am moving toward the attainment of my goals and patience and success surround me.

You may be thinking, "Okay, I'll say these things, but I don't believe them." This is only normal, especially if you're tired and haven't felt happy and hopeful in a long time. Don't give up. Even if you don't believe the positive statements or positive visualizations, keep saying them over and over. Because somewhere at the core of your person you believe, *or you wouldn't have bought this book!* You just lost touch with yourself, you didn't lose yourself—though it may seem like it! Another exercise to help break your Catch-22 is to do a little daydreaming.

DAYDREAMING

"You're daydreaming again!" Many of us grew up with the idea that daydreaming wasn't good. Children who were caught daydreaming were considered to have short attention spans, or possibly poor listening skills, and it was seldom viewed as a creative time. I never had a class in school called daydreaming, but I certainly would have gotten an "A".

It certainly would be interesting to have a class in school called creative daydreaming, and listen to the daydreams of adults and children freed from the restrictions of our intellect and the strong realities of life. Our minds will always fill themselves with thoughts, and most daydreams are passing thoughts that last only a few seconds.

Daydreaming is a way to relax and get rid of tension or feelings of restlessness by possibly creating a menagerie of pleasant positive thoughts. It is a great way to let go. This is a wonderful way to mentally act through your problems and rehearse solutions or reactions to future situations.

Daydreaming can help you get out of an unpleasant mood, because you have the freedom to bring into your mind any thought you want. You can increase your self-esteem by daydreaming, as you see yourself winning a race, or getting a new higher-paying job.

All in all it is up to you—start using your mind.

IT'S *YOU* THAT WORKS

It's *you* that works—not a diet or any number of gimmicks. The commercials on the "diet patches" claim that "the diet patch puts you in control, you don't have to stick with it—it sticks with you." What a gimmick! *You* create the controls needed to succeed, and one of those controls is patience. The diet patch has no power of its own, it is your hope and belief in it that works. I believe the most effective way to succeed is to give yourself enough time. Don't pick the fruit before it is ripe and then complain that it doesn't taste good. You weren't patient enough to give it time to taste as good as it could. Give yourself time to fully accept new beliefs as being lifelong, not just a means to an end. This change in itself—to learn to be patient and allow time for important changes—is challenging because we are not taught to be patient with change. If we fail, few of us think about trying it just one more time. Few of us have the confidence to take a new direction, accepting that what we thought would work didn't. Don't be afraid to say, "Oooops, I made a mistake," and then go on.

This self-honesty and extra effort is worth the ultimate freedom. Wanting everything right away with minimum effort is reinforced by our instant society. You are used to immediate results in many areas of your life, which affects you on a subconscious level. If you want a quick meal, there are fast food restaurants, or if you need gas, there are self-service stations to eliminate waiting in line. Gimmicks also promise instant results, with minimum effort. Taking a pill is much less work than it is to organize your time, and discipline yourself to eat healthily.

Give yourself time to discover yourself! Progress and happiness come a step at a time, and sometimes there isn't any immediate gratification. This is when you must zap yourself with a extra dose of patience and keep on going.

Usually a great deal of effort is required any time you start something new, and the more familiar you become with it the simpler it gets. Placing that first piece to a puzzle is much more difficult than the pieces following it. As you start to see the full picture, placing the pieces becomes easier! Give yourself time to become more familiar with your new behaviors. It may seem uncomfortable at first, just like a new hair style; it wasn't the hair style that you didn't like, but possibly the uncomfortable feeling of change itself.

There are no magical solutions! Either work hard to gain control of your eating problem, or continue to suffer. It is you that works! Trust yourself.

PROCRASTINATION: ANXIETY OF STAGNATION

So, you say you're a procrastinator, and just can't seem to get going? Well, a large number of people feel this way, so they think and think about why they are procrastinators, and a few years later they're still thinking. So many people think and think about their thinking, and then think about thinking about what they're thinking about! Stop thinking, and start doing something—anything.

Doing nothing but thinking produces anxiety. It is the anxiety of stagnation—the anxiety that comes from not doing anything but thinking and worrying about what you are supposed to do. Doing nothing requires more energy, because you're always worrying about what you should be doing! Eventually, all the worrying tires you out, and no change has occurred. Mental activity can tire you out as much as too much physical activity.

So don't further prolong your anxiety by trying to think and intellectually explain why you can't get going! Get rid of the idea that it is all or nothing. If you make even the smallest change, you're not going to experience the anxiety of stagnation. Even though you want to exercise every day, doing some type of exercise, even if it is only one day a week, is movement toward positive change.

Anytime you make a change with good intentions, no matter how small the change, or even if it doesn't work, you'll never feel as bad, because you know you tried.

Don't wait until you have to change, and feel you are going to lose something (health) you can't live without. The longer you wait, the more anxiety builds and builds until it finally turns into a fear. The fear develops into a feeling of panic—I've *got* to do it, I *can't*—and then ends again in procrastination. This is the cycle many tired dieters get on—the stagnation cycle.

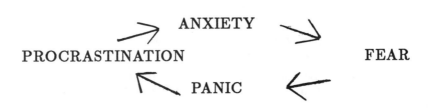

Wanting too much too soon can cause stagnation, because you're always starting over. Each time you start over, you're reminded of all the times you've failed in the past, and self-esteem gets lower and lower. With more patience, over time the anxiety of stagnation can be eliminated. Lastly, the "obstacle seeker" suffers also from the anxiety of stagnation.

THE OBSTACLE SEEKER

The obstacle seeker feels the anxiety of stagnation quite frequently. This is the person who finds constant obstacles to place in front of the things they know must be done. Obstacle seekers create "what if's-phobia." "What if it doesn't work," or "What if so-and-so gets mad." All these imagined "what if's" turn to anxiety, fear, and actual phobias. Obstacle seekers can take "what if's" and become stagnated over what may never happen. The obstacle seeker can use other people's problems or create problems for others out of fear of making changes in their own lives that may require them to face a truth or fear.

VALERIE

At age 34, Valerie was a diet expert, knowing all of the foods and the caloric values of every "forbidden" food, feeling helpless and guilty if these foods were even near her, because the temptation grew stronger. She was extremely disappointed in herself because she was always starting over, never fully succeeding in her efforts. Each time Valerie failed her anxiety grew, and eventually she went to have a medical checkup, thinking that there could be something biologically wrong. She had a TMA (trace mineral analysis) done, as well as urine and blood analyses, and a GTF (glucose tolerance test), along with triglyceride, uric acid, and cholesterol tests, HDL's, and LDL's.

Her tests proved her to be biologically fit, which made her feel even more anxious; she had been hoping for some physical malfunction to explain her inability to lose weight.

Valerie's only malfunction was her impatience with herself, never giving herself enough time or room for mistakes. If eating and exercising didn't turn out exactly as planned, she threw away all her plans. Even if she merely *thought* too frequently about her "forbidden food," guilt overwhelmed her and she quit!

Each week when we would set goals, she would make lengthy lists of goals to complete in an unrealistic time period. Even when Valerie complained that things weren't going right, they were—but just not fast enough for her. In time, she understood that the excess weight was not an underactive thyroid but an overactive impatience with herself. This attitude spread to other areas in her life too, and she became more relaxed mentally by losing the emotional weight of not trusting herself. She also lost 26 pounds of physical weight. She now sticks with her goals and continues to trust in them even when they don't go exactly as planned.

Friendships in Valerie's life began to improve. As she relaxed and became more patient with herself, it spilled over into her social life.

If you're like Valerie, needing to have all or nothing, start to make small changes. Wanting too much too soon causes the anxiety of stagnation and burnout. It may be that you have an overactive impatience, not a underactive metabolism.

RENEE

Renee came into my office with several pictures of how she once looked, and felt she would never look or be happy like that again. Rene was 26 and felt life was not worth living anymore. She became so anxious around food she developed a food phobia. There were times Renee felt so anxious that she could not swallow her food. Renee appeared to be in good *physical* condition, but not in very good *emotional* condition. She wore very tight clothes, revealing her solid, muscular body. She told me she wore these tight clothes to remind herself of her excess weight so that she wouldn't overeat. In other words, Renee's clothes even made her anxious. When men would look at her she felt they were looking at her fat, another anxiety which lead her to eating less and exercising more.

Fruit was all she was eating, and I stressed the importance of eating a variety of food to get a variety of nutrients. She exercised twice a day, as well as running five miles a day. She did this for about 2 weeks until she burned out, and then suffered even more from the anxiety of stagnation. She would go for weeks doing nothing, then suddenly become anxious and begin again taking her behavior to an extreme by overexercising and eating fruit. She felt out of control, which manifested itself in her *overcontrolled* way of eating and exercising.

One of my first concerns was that she relax, and we went through a few relaxation steps, emphasizing trust and compassion for herself, giving back to her the control she had lost. Weighing herself was completely stopped, and she became much more relaxed, learning to listen to her feelings and pay more attention to her body, not the scale, and realizing that she did in fact look good.

Renee's trust in me helped her begin to trust and listen to herself. As she began to relax, we brought into sessions the foods she had developed phobias about. Renee ate these foods and learned that it was not the food that was the problem, but what she was *feeling* when eating. She learned not to eat when feeling anxious or

in a negative mood state. Changing her associations
with food took place over many months. By reducing
her exercising to every other day, she felt more relaxed
and in control. Overexercising for Renee was a signal
that she was not in control. All of her anxious demands
and negative thoughts were redirected toward a gentle
and confident caring for herself.

LUCY

Lucy was frantic and anxious about getting help,
and told me she knew what her problem was, but didn't
know how to stop it. She said, "No one knows why
I'm so overweight, because I purposely don't eat around
them." Lucy felt guilty eating in front of people and
now was feeling guilty about keeping secret her private
binging. She was about 60 pounds overfat, and felt
people were thinking, "What is she eating for? She's
got enough fat to live off of for ten years." The fact that
Lucy now felt guilty about hiding her secret binging was
a sign she was getting healthier and was able to see her
behavior more objectively. This was Lucy's first step to
recovery.

Lucy would binge late at night not on junk food, but
on good foods, so that she wouldn't feel so bad about
her binging. She hid certain foods in her cabinets, and
at the office a candy machine was conveniently located
down the hall. She strategically planned the proper
time to visit the candy machine, and even scouted out
the hall to see when the coast was clear! Then, by
carrying the correct change, she was able to quickly
insert the money before anyone saw her. Knowing what
lever to pull, she would immediately stuff the candy into
her pocket, saving it for a private moment.

Because Lucy felt eating the candy bar was the
ultimate sin, she anxiously consumed it as quickly as
possible, usually in the ladies' room. Lucy always hid

while eating these "bad" foods, adding to the anxiety of the ultimate sin. Eating so quickly because of the overwhelming guilt never gave her the time to enjoy or taste the creamy milk chocolate. All the food she ate was consumed in a hurry and not enjoyed. Therefore, she needed to eat more in hopes of gaining pleasure at some point.

One of Lucy's first steps was to stop labeling food good or bad, and to recognize that just because some foods do have lower nutritional value, they're not bad foods. Labeling foods caused more anxiety and guilt, and preoccupation with wanting to binge on them. The next step was to eat the candy bar in the office were everyone could see her eating, and eat with her family and friends. Lucy began to lose physical weight immediately, no longer eating as much food as she did during private binges. She was no longer feeling the guilt and negative feelings when eating. Food started to be more satisfying, because Lucy was eating more slowly and *tasting* her food, experiencing fullness and pleasure. Now that the candy bar wasn't a bad food, she didn't crave it anymore. If she ate one it was okay—she was in control.

These steps were given time and patience to work. They were new behaviors and Lucy cared enough for herself to work through them and take as much time as she needed. Placing a time limit on herself would have caused anxiety.

GETTING STARTED

The toughest time and greatest effort for both Renee and Lucy was at the beginning. Getting started is the toughest part about changing, because you have to be totally self-motivated, until you experience some success, and positive reinforcement! Until then you're on your own. This is why it is helpful to realize that getting help doesn't mean you are weak. You can still be strong and need someone to help you along. I help people learn to listen to themselves, trust what they are hearing, and make positive changes. It can be difficult to understand yourself and your behaviors objectively, and it is easy to feel stuck. Much like getting stuck in a snowstorm, you can get the car out, but may need some help, so you accept the help and get back on the road.

A POWERFUL MEDICINE: SETTING GOALS

Stop thinking so much, and set some small goals. They will give you the confidence and reinforcement for bigger goals later on. Goals keep you directed and help you set your boundaries. This requires being able to say No, or get motivated when things look bleak. Don't just think about them—write them down! When you do, they go from being a dream to becoming a goal, a far more tangible and specific endeavor. I'm always asked if I use pills or injections to help people overcome their eating problems, and I tell them that I do use a powerful medicine: *setting goals*. You must set your goal and then take positive action—just do it!

If you don't set goals, you'll always find a reason to delay getting started, and you start to feel the anxiety of stagnation. The more goals you set and accomplish, the more you increase your confidence and ability to make better choices and direct your life. Goals will keep you from procrastination, and from feeling out of control or becoming an obstacle seeker. They give you a base to work from. Just like building a house, you need to get a solid base established first; you don't just put in the windows. First things first. Take some small actions on your goals each day, so you don't become anxious and overwhelmed.

Never forget: The only one that stops you from achieving your goals is you! Give yourself time to succeed, and to understand and overcome behaviors and habits that have been in your life for a long time. There are also certain conditioned behaviors that you need to become aware of if you are to overcome your eating problem.

CONDITIONING

You do many things in your life for which you may not be aware of the motivations. You have been conditioned to behave in certain ways, and sometimes you're not even aware this conditioning has taken place. Think about, for example, the universal conditioning that happens at Christmas, when millions of people rush out to buy gift, even if they can't afford to do so! If you decide that you don't have the financial means, and you simply don't buy gifts, the guilt is overwhelming, to say the least! What about the times you have said, "Why did I do that?" or " I did that? I don't remember." Many times you act a certain way without conscious thought of doing so.

The process of *classical conditioning* can explain some of these occurrences. Classical conditioning is a process discovered by Ivan P. Pavlov, a Russian physiologist, in which a neutral stimulus was repeatedly paired with a reinforcer, which then came to elicit a response. An example of this theory can be applied to eating problems. Have you noticed how so many events are associated with eating? What's the first thing that comes to mind when you hear the word "Birthday"? Probably "Cake!" Christmas? Cookies. Valentine's Day? Candy. This is classical conditioning. The word "birthday" is the neutral stimulus and is paired with a reinforcer "cake," which then comes to elicit the response: eating.

A lot of people would feel very disappointed by not having a birthday cake. Can you go to a movie theater and not have popcorn? If you can, you have broken through the conditioning, which the movie theater owners hoped you'd just accept as normal. With every movie there is popcorn! With every birthday, there is cake. Classical conditioning is in effect as you hear a television commercial for the fifteenth time. You are not even aware that information is being stored for use the next time you go shopping. Popular soft drinks are paired with reinforcers such as sun-filled fun, excitement, and great looking bodies! All these conditioned thoughts make the product desirable, without you really knowing the motivation behind it.

Bringing this to awareness helps you to break the conditioned response, and buy on a *conscious* level. Remember this the next time you want to reward yourself for doing well and accomplishing a goal. Don't let your reward be counterproductive. Allow the feeling of satisfaction and peace of mind to be your reinforcer, and the elicited response to be your further success. In time you can condition yourself to elicit a response of healthy eating and thinking! Next, I want you to also condition yourself to get enough sleep, so you can continue to elicit positive healthy responses. When you are tired everything seems more difficult.

SLEEP TIME: RECHARGING TIME

What I'm going to say next may seem unusual, but you need to get enough sleep when making changes. Even positive changes can cause stress and demand more sleep time. Now, don't just say, "But I just don't have the time." Getting a good restful sleep makes you 100% more productive in your waking hours.

When going through changes, sleeping is sometimes more difficult because of the anxiety and excitement of change. This is when relaxation techniques and the lighter approach previously discussed should be used every day! Starting an exercise program is stressful and demands more sleep until the body adjusts to the extra energy needed. Once the body adjusts, exercise can boost, rather than deplete, energy. Sleep allows you to recharge yourself!

Sleep has been proven to be essential to mental health, and REM (rapid eye movement) is why. It is your REM stage of sleep that serves as an information-processing period in which data from the previous waking cycle are processed, sorted, and stored. REM sleep is essential to memory, mood, and alertness. When a child becomes irritable, many parents have them take a nap, and upon waking the child seems to have grown wings! Taking a nap is a terrific idea for children, and if corporations had sleep time for their employees around midday, morale and productivity would probably increase, even though an hour was lost for sleep. REM is the stage of sleep where dreaming and creative ideas are formed. Maybe corporate executives should take a snooze if a solution to a problem doesn't surface. Once you relax, the answer surfaces! Take the time to get the sleep you need, and recharge yourself!

CHAPTER FOUR: THINGS TO REMEMBER

* When you feel yourself growing impatient, start to care more for yourself.

* Permanent change takes more time and patience, and the feeling of deserving. Your self-honesty and extra effort are worth the ultimate freedom.

* Pushing and forcing change ensure only one thing—burnout.

* Deal with your simmering emotions before they boil over. Ask yourself, "What emotions are simmering within me?"

* You may not be able to forget certain experiences or people, but you can forgive.

* Your experiences, good and bad, were meant to be. Learn from them and then go on.

* Take one of your goals and use positive visualization to create the steps needed to control, overcome obstacles, and clearly see success with your goal.

* Start daydreaming, mentally acting through your problems and rehearsing solutions or reactions to future situations.

* It is you that works, not a diet or any number of gimmicks. Trust yourself!

* Get rid of the idea of all or nothing. Even the smallest change will eliminate the anxiety of stagnation.

* Don't be an obstacle seeker, creating for "what-if" phobias.

* Eat when you're relaxed, not anxious or in a negative mood state.

* Redirect your anxious thoughts toward a gentle and confident caring for yourself.

PART II

LOOKING AT BODY

Your health is your responsibility

and

Freedom comes with responsibility

— Doug Poppenger

5

Acquire the Habit of Health

It's time to realize that good health is not something to be taken for granted but, instead, an ongoing process that needs constant reinforcement. Your health is your responsibility, not the doctor's, and your health shouldn't be left to chance.

Eating problems are not just a female problem. Men can have eating problems too, such as anorexia, bulimia, or obesity. Anyone at any age can have an eating problem. During times of stress or change, when a person is feeling vulnerable, turning to or away from food for comfort and control is very common. Dancers, entertainers, models, athletes, and flight attendants are even more prone to having eating problems due to the emphasis placed on their appearance.

I have counseled hundreds of men and women with eating problems and have noticed a pattern. Men tend to lean toward excessive exercise and use of laxatives. Women, on the other hand, tend to lean toward food restriction, binging, and purging. Although it varies from individual to individual, this pattern does exist.

TREAT YOUR BODY WITH RESPECT

Let's get in the habit of health. To do so, you must treat your body with respect through the use of prevention. Think about a good friendship you have. That friendship grew as you and your friend began to understand one another, and then it grew even more as that understanding led to respect! This same idea can be applied to your health. You must first understand your body or you'll never learn to respect it! In the first few chapters you learned to understand yourself emotionally; now you need to understand your body! You've been stating to yourself that, "I care about myself." Now start adding, "I care about my body."

If I were to ask you what two things you want most out of life, you'd probably say your health and then— oh, a couple million dollars! Yet you realize that it doesn't matter how much money you have because without your health you have absolutely nothing. Now, even though you know this to be true, why then do you find it so difficult to take care of your health? You want to maintain good health but you find it difficult to make the extra effort or necessary sacrifices for it. If you're saying to yourself, "I just don't have the time, to eat right and exercise," then realize you must make a few switches in your priorities and use that time for your health. If not, your poor eating and lack of exercise will eventually force you to make a change. This is not the way to make change! This is why so many people view change as so difficult: because they wait until they *have to* change, and that makes it harder and more frightening. Your heart and lungs can improve with as little as fifteen minutes of vigorous exercise three times a week. Don't say it's all or nothing. Doing something *will* improve your health.

You work so hard to get ahead in life, sometimes at the expense of your health, only later to pay a bigger price once your body falls subject to disease or illness.

The body will always try to produce health, and once it breaks down, it's usually because it has been abused past its own ability to fend for itself. It's your body. Stay in touch with it, or it will reflect your lack of attention through poor health. I meet a lot of people who are subconsciously angry with their body, because they used to be able to eat a lot more food and have a lot more energy, and now they wonder why their body let them down. These people just keep on hoping that one day their body will pop back to what it used to be, and meanwhile stubbornly insist on not making positive changes. Your body is constantly changing, and you must listen and accept those changes.

This chapter will help you understand your body and how it functions, and how to care for it by making positive changes. Everyone has different capabilities, and there is no one fitness or caloric prescription that fits everyone. I truly believe that the better you understand something, the more you can believe in it and thereby overcome your eating problem.

If you want to overcome your eating problem, you must first understand how your body functions so you can respect it by being patient. For example, the better you understand how fat is burned, the more you'll see the hazards of magic creams, diet pills, laxatives, dieting, diet drinks, and especially fasting, which is a dangerous dietary measure causing hypotension and dehydration, as well as electrolyte imbalance. Electrolytes are minerals, such as potassium, sodium, calcium, magnesium, and phosphate.

Understanding how fat is burned and how your body functions, you'll no longer try to blow off 10 pounds in a week, and you'll understand the physical dangers. When physical weight is lost too quickly, the body experiences symptoms of semi-starvation, and will actually hold onto fat. Eventually your body will return to its set point, which wasn't given time to change, the physical weight returns, and emotional weight increases.

If a person weighs 165 pounds and loses 35 pounds in just a couple of weeks, their set point is still at 165. Once their obsessive way of eating and exercising stops, the body will work at going back to the set point of 165. The body sees fat as survival. If you try to get rid of it too quickly, you're not respecting your body but threatening its survival, and it will fight back by returning to set point weight.

Do you still think that a protein diet is better than eating carbohydrates? How do carbohydrates, protein, and fat work, and how much should you eat? We all need the same nutrients, but in different amounts, depending on age, growth, size, stress, and activity level. We all lose fat from different areas of the body. Just because you want to lose fat from your right thigh, that doesn't mean your body will cooperate. Fat comes from a pool of lipids (fatty acids) throughout your body, not always from the specific area you desire, and you may have a greater predisposition to lay down fat in certain areas. Fat is burned in every cell of your body, but primarily in your muscle tissue. Fat can't be dissolved or forced out of the fat cell with fat-burning pills; it must be burned in your muscle tissue. You don't just don't wake up one morning and find fat neatly piled next to your bed, so you can easily dispose of it. I'm sure you've heard the commercials on "Burn Fat As You Sleep." This is wishful thinking in its purest form!

Even though your main concern is to achieve a good physical body weight as quickly as possible, ultimately your goal should be to be happy, healthy, and in control of eating, which means starting a healthy exercise and eating menu, as well as a menu for keeping a positive strong attitude.

FORCED TO CHANGE

Don't wait until you're sick to become health wise. Taking care of yourself is a choice of wisdom. It is easy to use your intellect to make excuses and brush aside your emotions—until you are forced to change, flooded with emotions like fear and regret. Prevention is a form of wisdom. It is treating wellness. For many people, treating illness is the way they take care of their health. Start now, while you still have a choice. It is a known fact that your health depends much more on your ability to prevent disease than to treat illness once it has occurred. Start developing preventive health measures (treating wellness); don't wait until you've been frightened into taking care of yourself because you were diagnosed as having high cholesterol. Once this occurs, you no longer feel you have a choice, you've been told you have to care for your health. You then can become fanatical and overly preoccupied with your health because your motivation was "fear induced."

Eventually, you burn out, and anger, regret, fear, guilt, and resentment turn inward as a means of self-punishment. I've seen this happen time and time again as people do the complete opposite of what the doctor or health professional advises. The feelings of having to and wanting to improve health have two different meanings. You have freedom of choice, so why not choose to *want* to respect and take care of your body? Get rid of the excuse that it is not the right time, or you're too busy to exercise or eat healthy. Being too busy to care for your body means you're out of control.

I've talked to hundreds of people who have lost physical weight because they are "too busy to eat." Yet as soon as they have enough time to eat, they regain their physical weight and return to the original set point, once again feeling defeated when it comes to eating. Food wasn't the cause of their defeated feeling. It was the way they went about trying to lose physical weight. These are the same people who tell me that food has a "power" over them, but they don't understand that *they* are the ones giving food its power! You're giving food its power, and you can change this feeling of helplessness by applying discipline, organization, consistency, and moderation to your way of thinking.

ALL YOU CAN EAT!

There is no such thing as a free lunch. "All you can eat"—or should I say devour—is no bargain. Yes, you're saving money but ruining your body. Stuffing yourself to ensure you're getting your $6.95 worth means you'll pay more in medical costs down the road. This is the time you should respect and save your body, not your pocketbook. This again is using your wisdom and looking into the future, and not falling subject to immediate gratification. Going to an "all you can eat" restaurant is like jumping into quicksand, if you've been "dieting." You are hungry and can use your intellect to rationalize why eating everything and as much as you want is okay—because you've been good all week! You'll know you've lost control completely when you start eating things you don't even like!

HOW TO AVOID OVEREATING

This is what you can do. Take a deep breath and breathe out—try not to blow anything off the table! Exhale gently and think the word *calm*. Eating is a way you can relax and calm down, so fill your mind with the word *calm* in place of food. Controlling your eating means controlling your mind. Bring into your mind the fact that you don't have to overeat because tomorrow you will also eat. Don't bargain with yourself by saying, "I'll eat now and not tomorrow." This just leads to overeating for at least a week until you again punish yourself by avoiding food.

Does this sound familiar?

If you continue to restrict food and then eat when you can no longer override your own body's urges you will always fear losing control around food. Bring to your mind the word *calm* and then visualize yourself eating certain foods and in moderation, and being in control. After your visualization, ask yourself how you feel. Then work through those feelings before you eat. If you need help to work through these feelings, ask for help—it shows strength!

Relax and calm down before you eat to avoid what I earlier referred to as eating in a negative mood state. When you first come home, relax, make a cup of tea; don't just start randomly inhaling food because you still have not calmed down. When you're eating don't have a lot of outside noise blasting in your ear, like the TV. Watching the 6:00 news can cause a lot of stress that you're not even aware of. I'm sure you find yourself saying, "What? Oh no! I don't believe it, that's terrible!"

Here's another method you can use that works, if you tend to overeat. Close your eyes and visualize yourself eating the foods you are presently desiring. In your mind eat the food and let yourself really experience it: focus on taste, color, smell, and the feeling of fullness. Then ask yourself, "How do I feel after eating all this food?" You'll probably find yourself feeling quite relieved that this experience occurred in your mind. This experience is similar to having a dream and waking up relieved that it was just a dream—yet it seemed so real. Your mind is powerful. If it can convince you to eat, it can also do the opposite and help you apply moderation, not food restriction.

If you can't eat when you're upset, sit down and take some nice deep breaths—thinking the word *calm*. Have a bowl of soup or something else light, but by all means eat! You need the nutrients to help you deal with what is bothering you. Don't allow your emotions to affect how you eat! Separate them, so no matter what you are feeling, your eating stays healthy and regular.

As emotions fluctuate, food should not. You can do it. Practice.

If you are a busy person with an active lifestyle, then take even better care of your body to ensure that you can continue to live your life to the fullest! A person who doesn't like their life and themselves can never find a reason to care for their body. Start caring, and you'll be amazed at how it will help you a find reason to continue to care! This is what is meant by loving yourself.

My ultimate objective is to help you see what an incredible mechanism your body is and that you need to care for it or it won't take care of you! It's that simple. The more you know about nutrition and how your body functions, the less you will rely on the scale to tell you how successful you are. You'll listen more to how you feel. Remember, the scale only tells you how many *pounds* lost, not how much *fat* is lost. It weights fat as well as lean body mass such as muscles, bones, and internal organs. You could lose 20 pounds, with 10 pounds of it being protein from lean muscle tissue. As you learn to understand how your body works, you'll have more respect for it and you'll stop abusing it through poor eating habits and no exercise.

APPRECIATE YOUR BODY

When you look in the mirror, it would be great if you could take a look inside just like you can look at yourself on the outside and say, " Gosh! I look tired." Once your body starts to show bad effects on the outside you've been in trouble on the inside for quite a while! Your liver, for instance, weighs about four pounds, and has the ability to modify just about any chemical structure if kept healthy. When you don't consume enough carbohydrates, protein, fat, and other nutrients, or consume too much processed, adulterated food, or drink

too much alcohol, you are making your liver work over-
time.

The essential nutrient, protein, is composed of a variety of amino acids. Amino acids contain carbon, hydrogen, oxygen, and nitrogen. If your body has a lack of
one particular amino acid, the liver will take the nitrogen from another amino acid and combine it with some
of the carbon, hydrogen, and oxygen elements found in
carbohydrates or fats to make the protein that is lacking. In other words, as much as you continue to abuse
your wonderful body, it will try to compensate for a
lack of a particular nutrient.

You can only abuse your body for so long before this
incredible mechanism will no longer work for you. The
liver has many intricate functions. It produces enzymes,
vitamin A from carotene, vitamin D, and glycogen. It is
also involved in bile production (emulsification of fats)
and the blood coagulation factor. This is just the function of one organ! It's incredible how the body is taken
for granted, to just do its job even when it is abused—
that's loyalty! Thousands of people abused their bodies
with the popular but dangerous high-protein diet, not
realizing the risk of possible cardiac arrhythmia (irregular heartbeat), or loss of calcium, potassium, phosphorus, sodium, etc. A lot more than just physical weight
was lost. Some people even lost their lives!

BALANCING THE BODY

You have a unique biological individuality and must
find what works best for you. There are a few healthy
guidelines that you can follow and use as stepping stones
to find what is right for you.

Now, just what is a balanced diet? Most balanced
diets I see are in a textbook, but are rarely seen on
people's dinner tables.

A balanced diet means you select correct proportions from the four basic food groups. For adults, this consists of two servings from the meat group, two servings from the milk group, four servings from the fruit and vegetable group, and four servings from the grain group. The four food groups contain what are called "nutrient-dense foods," whereas junk foods are "empty calorie foods" that lack nutrient density. The next time you want to eat something, ask yourself, "Is this a nutrient-dense food?"

The recommended serving size for the four food groups provides an average of 1200 calories for women and not less than 1800 calories for men.

DESTRUCTIVE CALORIES?

Let's clear up some faulty thinking about calories. Food was put on this earth to keep us alive and to help us achieve optimal health.

Don't think of calories as destructive—they are not. The word "calorie" shouldn't send a fearful chill through your body!   Calories express the amount of energy supplied by food, and energy needs are met by carbohydrates (sugar, starches), proteins, fats, and alcohol. Ounce for ounce, carbohydrates and protein supply the same number of calories (four per gram), whereas fats supply more than twice as many (nine calories per gram). You may eat a six-ounce piece of beef, having 500 calories, but the protein may account for only 140 calories, the remainder being fat. Don't think of beef or chicken as 500 destructive calories, but as a good healthy food.

This is why I don't believe in weighing foods before you eat, because that particular food is then thought of as a destructive calorie instead of a good food!

ALL CALORIES ARE NOT CREATED EQUAL

Because all calories are not created equal, calorie counting is a waste of time, and food shouldn't be viewed in terms of calories.

Eating 1000 calories of whole grains, fish, chicken, or fruit and vegetables isn't the same as eating 1000 calories in cookies, ice cream, cake, and candy, even though they both total 1000 calories.

It is not only the number but the kinds of calories you eat that matters. This is because foods are absorbed differently. You may eat a piece of cake (simple carbohydrate) that contains 135 calories, or two pieces of whole wheat bread (complex carbohydrates) that also contain 135 calories. The whole wheat bread is a complex carbohydrate with more nutrient density like iron, B vitamins, calcium, and fiber, and is absorbed much more slowly, allowing your body more time to burn the food before storing it as fat for later use. The cake is absorbed quickly because white sugar has no nutrient density like vitamins and minerals and is more likely to be stored as fat if the body can't use this sudden food for energy.

Such *simple* carbohydrates are *simply,* or rapidly, absorbed from the intestinal tract and sent to the liver in amounts too large for the liver to store. Some simple carbohydrates are candy, sugar, cake, cookies, soft drinks, white bread, and white rice; these are foods that contain few nutrients. *Complex* carbohydrates (starches, fiber) are absorbed more slowly and don't overload the liver. The liver then releases them into the blood, and they go directly to the heart, which pumps them all over the body. As they go through the pancreas, insulin is secreted, taking sugar out of the blood.

Fructose (fruit sugar) and sucrose (table sugar) are in a more simple form than the sugars found in vegetables and grains. Complex carbohydrates like whole grains, vegetables and whole fruits are composed of sugars linked together in such a way that the breakdown process takes longer than simple or refined carbohydrates, and are absorbed more slowly into the bloodstream, therefore not stimulating a large rise in insulin levels. Simple carbohydrates break down rapidly, and absorption takes just a few minutes, creating a quick rise in blood sugar, unlike complex carbohydrates, which provide a gradual blood sugar increase that may take several hours.

This is why calories are not equal. Out of the four food groups, the cereal and fruit and vegetable groups are the two primary contributors of carbohydrates in the diet.   Some foods in the milk and meat group also contain moderate amounts of simple and complex carbohydrates—like milk and ice cream.

UNDERSTANDING THE DIFFERENCE: BRAIN AND MUSCLE FUEL

There are three main components the body uses for fuel: carbohydrates, proteins, and fats. Carbohydrates (simple and complex) are used for energy because they are quickly converted to glucose, which is the body's main fuel, especially for the brain. Protein can be converted into glucose by the liver if needed when you're not getting enough carbohydrates. Protein, however, should not be used for fuel, but for cell growth, repair, and maintenance. If you are not eating enough carbohydrates it can cause the breakdown of protein from the lean muscle tissue, as well as from the liver, heart, and kidneys. As your muscles get smaller, your ability to burn fat decreases. Therefore, the more muscle you have, the more fat you will burn and the more calories you can eat. Carbohydrates prevent the breakdown of protein so it can serve its function.

You can become overfat by eating too much protein just as you can by eating too many carbohydrate foods.

Make sure you are eating a good amount of complex carbohydrates, like potatoes, brown rice, pasta, whole wheat bread, fruits, vegetables, legumes, dried peas, beans, and lentils. Use the protein to build the muscle and burn the fat. Remember, fat is burned primarily in the muscle tissue.

Eat in limited amounts foods like bakery goods, candy, soft drinks, sugared cereals, white flour, white sugar, and polished rice, which are all simple or refined carbohydrates.

The more of the refined carbohydrates you eat, the more B vitamins you need, because these foods are high in flavor and low in nutrients. B vitamins are important to the metabolism of carbohydrates, fats, and proteins.

Even milk contains lactose (milk sugar), and the enzyme lactase is needed to digest lactose. If you lack this enzyme you may not be able to digest milk or some milk products that contain lactose without experiencing stomach discomfort. This is called being lactose intolerant, and it is not life-threatening, just uncomfortable.

I suggest you have a healthy balance of nutrients, with carbohydrates consisting of 65-70% (with 10% of that being simple carbohydrates and the rest complex) of total calories, protein 20-25%, and fats 10%. This is just a guideline and can vary from individual to individual, depending on age, height, weight, health, mental activity activity level, and physique. Too much or too little of any of these nutrients can be destructive to your body, because you need a balance of all these nutrients. Let's say you consume your caloric need of 1200 calories with a nutrition drink that contains a balance of carbohydrates, proteins, fats, vitamins and minerals, and you still feel hungry. Why? The nutrition drink was well balanced, and did meet your calorie requirement.

You were missing a few important factors like chewing, tasting, and the filling of your stomach, which are necessary if you want to feel satisfied. On the other hand, a unbalanced diet can give you enough calories but still leave you hungry. Consuming 3000 calories in the form of simple carbohydrates is over your caloric intake of 1200, yet you're still hungry. This was not balanced and lacked the protein, fat, vitamins, and minerals needed to make you feel satisfied. Start counting nutrients, not calories, and you'll begin to understand much more about your body and the food you feed it!

There are many dangers that can come from unbalanced eating habits. When too much protein and too little carbohydrate are consumed, ketone bodies are produced and can cause ventricular arrhythmia and possible death. Let me explain further.

KETOSIS

Keeping the body balanced is important, and when in a state of ketosis it is dangerously out of balance. Ketosis is a metabolic fat-burning state. At low levels ketones are harmless and come from low carbohydrate intake. However, when severe restriction of carbohydrate occurs because you're "dieting," your liver is alerted that the carbohydrate is running out. Your body then overuses your stored fat to produce energy in your muscles and ketone bodies for your cerebral cells (brain). Thus, fat is being broken down for energy faster than the body can use it, and the liver releases ketones into the blood, causing acid blood, after it metabolizes the fatty acids.

Ketones suppress the appetite, which is why dieters say they don't even feel like eating if they have been severely restricting food. Ketones cause sleeplessness, hyperalertness, and the smell of acid breath. Many "dieters" have bad breath, and now you know why. Your body is in a state of starvation, and is desperately consuming its own fat reserve. The more you threaten your body the harder it will fight back, by storing more fat once you start eating healthy, well balanced meals.

The reason that high-protein, low-carbohydrate diets became and still are dangerously popular is the loss of weight the nervous dieter notices almost immediately. The loss of weight is not from fat but from the large amounts of water the body draws from the tissues to get rid of the overload of ketones and nitrogen in the body. This water loss can cause dehydration, muscle weakness, and loss of some valuable minerals. Face it, the weight lost in those "lose weight fast" programs is the loss of water weight and glycogen, which is a stored carbohydrate in the liver and muscle. Not fat! The marketers of these programs realize most people are impatient and want to see quick result even is not a valid result.

Not going on these types of "fast, destroy-your-body" programs isn't even a matter of intelligence, but has more to do with being patient. It is your lack of patience that keeps these programs in full bloom! A good way to break this need for quick results is to rely on indicators other than the scale. Ask yourself, "How do I feel?" "Have I been doing my best?" "How do my clothes fit?" "Do I have more energy and endurance?" Try measuring your waist, hips, thighs, and arms every month or so. Hopefully, there will be a decrease in inches and an increase in patience! Or learn to like your body—just the way it is!

EAT SLOWLY

Did you ever wonder why you're told to set your silverware down in between bites, or to eat slowly? Understanding why you are doing something helps you stay motivated and stick with your new behavior, like eating more slowly, for more than just a couple of meals. The reason for eating slowly is to allow the brain to release the hormone cholecystokinin (CCK), which causes you to stop eating. This release of CCK occurs when food enters the intestine (duodenum). So you want to eat slowly enough to allow the release of this hormone before you have consumed too much food. Are you eating fast because you feel guilty about eating, so you quickly devour your food? Slow down and enjoy what you are eating, and be thankful it is so abundant.

Listen to your body, or should I say your brain! There is a master gland called the hypothalamus located in your brain that controls your appetite and body temperature. A lot of overeating comes from not listening to yourself, and then going to the corner drugstore to buy something to control your appetite. These appetite suppressants just make you nervous and irritable. You have already been given a weight control mechanism, so save your money and buy some fresh, wholesome foods!

STOP BORING YOUR TASTE BUDS

You certainly wouldn't wear the same clothes every day, because you would get bored and tired of the same old thing. If you don't eat a variety of foods, you bore your taste buds to death! Variety keeps your taste buds stimulated and happy, not bored. Are your taste buds bored and lonely for a change to something new and flavorful?

Include a variety of tastes and textures, and prepare dishes that are visually appealing—colorful and attractive. If you eat the same food day after day, and then unexpectedly eat something with more flavor and appeal at a social function, your taste buds go *crazy with pleasure!* There are so many nutritious and wonderful foods available. It is only lack of knowledge and lack of taking the time to eat healthy foods that cause people to continue to eat the same old thing. A chicken omelet in the morning, chicken sandwich in the afternoon, and to top it off chicken casserole in the evening. Maybe we are indeed creatures of habit!

Try not to eat the same food more than once every four days. Even though you may love peanut butter and it is a healthy nutritious food, eating it every day does not provide you with a balance of essential vitamins, minerals, and proteins that are found in other foods. Making sure you eat a variety of foods keeps your interest in eating healthy and keeps you healthier by supplying you with all the nutrients you need for optimal health.

This is why I do not believe in diet drinks or eating special nutrition bars as a meal replacement. It is just another costly, temporary behavior that won't lead to permanent change, but just leave you tired and once again disappointed, and as we discussed earlier— hungry! You need to chew food, and listen to it crunch, and feel satisfied and comfortable—not stuffed.

Eat slowly and ask yourself. "Do I feel comfortable?" Don't wait until you have to loosen your clothing, or lay down because you are too full, or feel you need an oxygen tank to breathe. Over the holidays it's the turkey you're suppose to stuff—not yourself! Your body is talking to you all the time—listen to it! Listening to your body means eating regular meals, and when you skip meals you stop listening, and are overriding your own body process—its need for nourishment!

Understanding Your Body

Are you feeling tired all the time, even after a good night's sleep? Do you feel dizzy and can't seem to concentrate? Does your breath smell bad from ketosis? Are constipation and gas a problem because of poor digestion and nutrient uptake? Having an anxious or a nervous kind of energy can cause indigestion or gas, as you unconsciously swallow more air because you're taking shallow, more frequent breaths and eating faster. The fizz of a fresh soda pop reacts in much the same way inside your body. Pop, pop, fizz, fizz—as the carbonation warms up in the body and carbon dioxide is produced and fills you up with gas, it's not FAT! Thinking of this bloated feeling as being FAT is a common reaction when you're a chronic dieter who naturally overreacts to the littlest change in your body.

Trying to get rid of this bloated feeling by restricting food only worsens the problem by not getting the nutrients you need to get rid of your discomfort. Not eating may give you temporary psychological relief, but it worsens your biological distress! Just because diet pop or any other food has only one calorie doesn't mean it's good for you.

Do you have muscle cramping, headaches, or mood swings, or do you feel cold a lot? When you start restricting food your body will sacrifice heat and energy for survival. If you're binging and purging, your esophagus may feel sore and swollen, and your cheeks may swell. The purging of food causes the loss of valuable nutrients, and physical signs appear like thinning, brittle hair, dry skin, complexion problems, and dark rings and bags under the eyes. All these are signals to you that your body is hurting, like a child crying for help!

Getting the proper nutrients is essential to overcoming any problem in life, especially eating problems. You need to have the mental and physical strength to change. Vitamins and minerals are essential to overcoming your eating problem, providing health for the many physiological functions in the body needed for you to recover. For example, achieving a good balance between potassium and sodium make possible the iodine pump; without it you can't produce thyroid hormone, which needs iodide. Thyroid hormone helps regulate glucose metabolism. This pump helps carry nutrients to the cells and waste products out! You need a nutrient-rich body to recover. Healthy digestion is necessary because this is where nutrients are absorbed. Digestion provides both the building block molecules needed by the cells and the fuel for body functions.

The process for recovery is emotionally stressful in itself, and poor eating habits add all kinds of biological stress you can do without. Next, I will discuss how to reduce this biological stress, so your body no longer cries for help, but glows with health! Even though you've been suffering for quite a while mentally and physically, this healthy glow of mind and body is possible, by applying consistency to your new healthy behaviors. When you're consistent, the body takes you seriously enough to make permanent healthy changes. It is like telling a child he can't do something but allowing him to do it every once in a while; he will never take you seriously enough to make a permanent change. Be consistent and persistent in learning about your body.

DON'T SKIP MEALS: HEALTHY SNACKING

Save yourself hundreds of dollars in fad gimmicks, and start applying a simple behavior pattern to your life. Don't skip meals. Begin eating smaller, more frequent meals. If you start your day by skipping breakfast, you aren't taking in fuel until noon each day, and then you are starving and out of control by lunchtime, and you overeat. If you want to lose fat and develop a healthy lean body weight, eat six smaller, more frequent meals.

I'm not saying you have to become Betty Crocker, or spend your life in the kitchen. There is a simple way to apply this way of eating without turning on a stove!

Extensive studies have been conducted on how the frequency of eating can affect how much of that food is stored as fat or burned as energy. A study was done in which the first group of people was given 250 calories to eat at breakfast, and 400 at lunch and 650 calories at dinner, for a total of 1300 calories. The second group was given the same exact foods but 100 calories fewer, but ate it all in two meals instead of three, skipping breakfast. Group one lost more fat, even though they consumed more calories, than the second group, which consumed fewer calories and lost no fat.

This is because eating smaller, more frequent meals gives your body time to burn those calories (fuel) for immediate energy or store them for energy in the liver and muscle as glycogen.

Eating large or even moderate amounts of food after allowing a longer period of time to pass between meals creates fuel without an energy need, and the fuel will be converted to fat until it is needed. When you eat, you're actually increasing the rate at which you burn calories (metabolic rate) by 10-35% and remain stimulated for the next 2-3 hours. The less food you eat, the fewer the calories you will burn. When you stop eating for long periods of time you have turned off your body, just like you turn off your car. When your car is running you're burning gas, and when you eat you are burning calories, through digestion, absorption, transport, and metabolism of nutrients from the food you ate. If you don't eat or eat only once a day, your body doesn't use the fuel needed for these processes. It just shuts down, and waits for a meal.

Snacking can help you keep burning calories, while keeping your blood sugar stable, helping to alleviate your midafternoon fatigue. Not eating for long periods of time causes your blood sugar to get progressively lower and can cause mild, moderate, or even severe hypoglycemia (low blood sugar). This creates such symptoms as fatigue, weakness, anxiety, and personality changes like irritability, sadness, and mood fluctuation. I have seen so many of these symptoms in people who are dieting and consuming very little food. Normal blood glucose levels are 80-100 milligrams of glucose per 100 milliliters of blood. If blood glucose gets too low you get the "Munchies" (sensation of hunger).

"Munching out" is overloading your system with foods high in sugar and fat, and when these foods enter the bloodstream, glucose levels will rapidly rise, triggering the release of excessive amounts of insulin from the pancreas. The parasympathetic nervous system stimulates the pancreas to release insulin so it can transport the glucose from the blood into liver, muscle, and fat cells. This may cause an overproduction of insulin (insulin removes excess sugar from the blood) as blood glucose levels fall too low again, and you need another "sugar fix." Have you ever been on this roller coaster ride, feeling high—and then real low? Having too much circulating insulin in your bloodstream can contribute to arteriosclerosis, because the insulin can cause fats to be deposited in the arterial walls. Munching out may be a little more serious than you think!

Hypoglycemia can be caused not only by infrequent eating and poor eating habits but by a tumor in the pancreas, causing overproduction of insulin or malfunction of the liver, which interferes with the storage of sugar. Studies have shown that coffee triggers the pancreas to release insulin, and that decaffeinated coffee disturbs blood sugar levels. Insulin is very important as a storage hormone that stimulates the accumulation of glycogen, triglycerides, and protein in the liver, fat, and muscle cells.

Therefore, insulin plays a part in how fat is stored in the fat cell. Insulin directs the storage of triglycerides inside the fat cells in the adipose tissue (fat tissue) for the purpose of storing fat to be used later when food becomes scarce. When glucose is high, this is called hyperglycemia. This is commonly seen in people who are diabetic and have inadequate insulin production.

When blood sugar gets too high, the kidneys transfer some of the sugar into the urine. Exercise for the diabetic is vital, because it uses sugar without the use of insulin, burning sugar as fuel.

COMMON SENSE SURVIVAL KIT

This may seem backwards, but the more you deprive your body of food (fuel) the more it will hold onto whatever you consume by storing it as fat, in fear of starvation. Don't let a long period of time pass between meals. Let's say you eat breakfast at 7:00, have a snack at 10:00, and then lunch at 12:30, and later another snack at 3:30, dinner at 6:00, and around 8:00 a bedtime snack. You're probably panicking by now, thinking, "This is impossible!" Let me explain what I mean by a snack, or what I like to call *Your Common Sense Survival Kit!* This means taking along with you in a bag or purse (or keeping a kit in your car) some pumpkin or sunflower seeds, dried unsulfured fruit mix, soybean nuts, peanuts, almonds, walnuts, raisins, a granola mixture without all the palm oil or coconut oil, and of course the faithful apple, carrot, or celery sticks. Be creative and eat these foods as your small snack, and don't bring the whole bag of nuts but place a limited amount in your kit.

These are good, nutritious foods and should be eaten in moderation, and will keep you burning calories throughout the day. If you stop eating, you stop burning calories—your body shuts down! As you can see, you don't have to eat a lot of food to keep your body turned on and blood sugar stable, so you don't lose control when you finally allow yourself the privilege of eating. You can also avoid getting tired by using snacks as a way to eat smaller, more frequent meals.

Having a snack before bedtime can help you burn more calories because the process of digestion, absorption, transport, and metabolism begins, all of which requires energy. Calories are units of energy; all these processes *burn calories!* If you are going to have a bedtime snack, don't eat something high in fat or sugar, because one hour after the onset of sleep there is a burst of growth hormone (GH) released from the anterior pituitary gland. It is the appetite control center—the hypothalamus—that tells the pituitary to release GH.

Growth hormone contains 191 amino acids (protein) and stimulates muscle growth and fat burning as well as maintaining the immune system and several other functions. Eating sugar and fat before bedtime stops the release of growth hormone from the pituitary. Can you see that healthy snacking is healthy for both your mind and body? Your energy needs are constant, and if controlling your eating means controlling your mind, it is important that you keep your brain furnished with energy, so you can make good decisions.

STOP FEELING TIRED AFTER EATING

Many people with eating problems feel tired all the time, starving themselves all day and then indulging in dinner, wanting to do nothing but sleep after eating. Food should give you energy—not tire you out! Eating only one indulging meal or eating until you're stuffed leaves you with a sluggish, tired feeling. Overloading your system this way causes blood flow to be directed to the stomach for digestion, and elevates blood triglycerides (blood fats), slowing oxygen delivery to the muscles and brain, causing fatigue and sluggishness. Triglycerides in the blood are much like glue in the blood, impairing oxygen transportation.

Ninety-nine percent of our fat in our fat cells is stored as triglycerides. When glucose or blood sugar enters the fat cell, it is converted to glycerol phosphate and is esterified with free fatty acids to form triglycerides. The fat cell is very elastic; it can hold small or large amounts of triglycerides, so every time you overeat the body adjusts to the excess by increasing the fat cell size.

Eating smaller, more frequent meals creates a regular flow of stored triglycerides to travel out of the fat cell. When you eat too much, your stomach gets overloaded and has trouble producing enough enzymes to completely break down the foodstuff, so the mass of food enters the small intestine and is too much to be absorbed and too much for your liver to handle.

You can't fool mother nature. Instead, understand your body and food, stop fooling around, and gain control.

YOU CAN'T FOOL MOTHER NATURE: BURNING FAT

Most of us at some time or another have said, "You're pushing me too far, and I won't be able to take it much longer." How many times do you think your body has communicated this same message to you, and you have just ignored it?

Your body sees fat as survival. When you lose fat too quickly or starve yourself and become dangerously thin, your body will try to store more fat by increasing fat cell size and number. If you're restricting food and/or binging or purging you're not fooling your body but threatening it, and it will fight back by increasing your fat cell number in hopes of storing more fat to keep you alive. You may have noticed how some people look terribly worn out after or during physical weight loss, having dark circles or puffiness under their eyes. These are signs that some important nutrients needed for energy and body maintenance are lacking. Potassium, for example, is found in high concentrations in your fat cells, so by losing fat you're also losing potassium. Did you know that fat has a rich blood supply? Fat has several miles of capillaries for every pound, so when you lose fat you're also losing iron. These are just a few reasons why some people look worn out after losing fat. This doesn't mean you should start taking mega- doses of these two minerals. Just make sure you get enough through your regular diet and reasonable supplements.

As long as your body has the strength to keep fighting for your health, it will. Once it no longer can, major signs of destruction from the inside start showing on the outside. Then the body begins to break down protein for energy, taking it from muscle tissue and even from the organs as they slowly wither away. By fasting more than 12- 24 hours, you're not losing fat but glycogen from your liver and muscles, and valuable vitamins and minerals. Maybe you're thinking, "This hasn't happened to me, and I've been dieting (or severely restricting food and or binging and purging)." Remember, your body remembers, and the damage accumulates, and symptoms could surface at any time! Stop pushing your body!

If you want to burn fat, you can't rush the process and then expect to keep your health and make a permanent change. Fat doesn't just go away all at once. You may recall earlier our discussion on how fats were stored with the help of insulin. I now want you to understand how fats are burned so you will be patient and helpful to your body so you can establish a healthy body weight, not a starving body weight!

This process takes time, as fats (fatty acids) are first mobilized from the fatty tissue where the triglycerides in the fat cells undergo hydrolysis to form fatty acids and glycerol, and are then released into the blood. Fatty acids are then transported to the muscle cells for release of energy or ATP. Fat is a major source of ATP (energy), and a good supply of oxygen is needed for fat to produce ATP (energy). This is why aerobics is fat burning, because aerobics means in the presence of oxygen!

If exercise becomes too intense, the fatty acids released from the fat tissue decrease, and the muscle cells rely more on carbohydrates—a quicker energy, not a longer-burning fat. This is your *anaerobic* cycle, which means in the absence of oxygen. This is when carbohydrates (sugars) are burned. Fat is burned throughout the body, but the majority of fat is burned in the muscle. Fat can't be converted to a carbohydrate (except for the glycerol of the fat, which produces very small amounts of carbohydrates) because acetyl CoA can't be converted to pyruvate. What I have just described to you may seem complicated but it is just more unfamiliar than complicated.

I want you to understand your body and care for it, by giving it time to do its work.

It is your muscle cells that contain the necessary enzymes to convert the energy for the fatty acids to a form that the muscles can use. The more muscle you have, the more fat you will burn, but if you are restricting food and nutrients you won't have the energy to exercise and increase your muscle mass. The creams advertised to burn fat are nothing but good hand creams.

If you've been trying to overcome your eating problem for a while I'm sure you've heard about the *basal metabolic rate* (BMR). Your basal metabolic rate is the amount of energy you use at rest. It is the rate at which your body needs energy for maintaining functions necessary for survival, like breathing, heart rate, blood circulation, body temperature—everything excluding digestion and activity. Your body also needs energy for activity and *specific dynamic action* (SDA), which is the energy needed to utilize food that is eaten. It includes digestion, absorption, transport, and metabolism. All these processes burn calories in order to perform their function. Calculating your BMR, SDA, and activity level, you can get a rough idea of how many calories you burn in one day.

The body needs a set number of calories each day to maintain a certain physical weight. This number varies, depending on age, body size, and activity level. You must burn 3500 calories to lose a pound of stored fat. If you want to lose one pound of fat a week, your food consumption must be reduced by 500 calories a day or you must expend enough energy to burn 500 calories per day, or do both as a combination. I suggest you eat in moderation and exercise more so you can gain the muscle you need to burn fat, which is not threatening to your body. When I help people lose physical weight I don't have them count calories. I have them listen to their body, which already has a weight regulating mechanism that needs to be turned on and listened to! You can learn how to reduce your food intake naturally.

There are numerous *anthropometric measurements* that can be used to determine fatty deposits in different parts of the body. In the Special K cereal promotion they ask you if you can pinch an inch. Try pinching a skinfold with your thumb and index finger over your abdomen or in the middle of the back of your upper arm. You should have between a half an inch and an inch to pinch.

More accurate is a skinfold caliper used at the triceps and subscapular skinfolds. The best of all measures is what I call the eyeball measure—simply look in the mirror. We have already discussed how emotional weight can effect the image reflected in the mirror, and that you must feel good inside to feel you look good outside. Scales, as well as height and weight tables, seem to frustrate people as they drive themselves toward a weight goal that may not be healthy. Compare several height and weight tables and you'll see many differences between them. They are too general. Should everyone who is a certain height all wear the same size shoe? Of course not! Try weighing yourself on three different scales. They will all come up with different numbers. It's like playing a slot machine, only you want lower numbers!

7

Appetite Suppressants

The diet didn't work again, and now you're desperate for the 15th time! You vaguely recall taking something that seemed to work—you think! Dashing off to the corner drugstore, you are amazed at the menagerie of diet pills. Now what? For the first two days you feel powerful and in control—you could be surrounded by gooey chocolate brownies and never flinch!

It's great, but in a deep dark corner of your mind you know it's not a healthy way to lose weight—but you've tried everything else, so what the heck! For four days you've gone to bed hungry and now you wake up and head straight to the kitchen, eating everything, even things you don't like! The diet pill isn't working anymore, so the next day you take two and can feel your heart and nerves racing and that out of control feeling is back. Does this sound familiar to some degree?

One of the most widely used of these often nerve-racking appetite suppressants is phenylpropanolamine hydrochloride (PPA). It is found in such products as Dexatrim, Anorexin, and Control. These suppressants work by temporarily increasing the brain's production of serotonin, a neurotransmitter in the brain responsible for appetite control. However, once you deplete the brain's supply of serotonin, the appetite suppressant no longer works, until your brain regenerates more serotonin.

Serotonin is also responsible for our ability to sleep. You may have difficulty sleeping when using appetite suppressants because they eventually deplete the brain of serotonin. Some side effects of appetite suppressants include nervousness, nausea, headaches, increased heart rate and irregular heartbeat. It is another temporary solution—not a healthy, positive change.

Caffeine is also added to these products, around 100-200 milligrams, which is about equal to two cups of coffee. Just as PPA is a stimulant, so is caffeine. Both raise blood pressure and excite the cortex of the brain, relieving fatigue. Caffeine also acts as a diuretic. In addition, caffeine seems to inhibit the enzyme that helps burn carbohydrates and that breaks down fats in the blood. An 8-ounce cup of coffee contains about 90-120 milligrams of caffeine per cup, and decaffeinated coffee has 1-6 milligrams.

Appetite suppressants are not wonder drugs, but produce their effects by stimulating your own brain chemicals. Some products even contain vitamins, minerals, and fibers such as methylcellulose, xanthan gum, and mucilages to give you bulk so you feel full. Yet most of us eat even when we feel full, and eat for many other reasons than simply hunger! Why not just buy some fruits, vegetables, and whole grains to get the bulk you need, as well as the nutrients not found in the bulking pill?

FAT HAS A MIND OF ITS OWN

Fat does have a mind of its own, and for the adolescent girl who starts to menstruate earlier, around the age of 10 or 11 it can be a frustrating time, as the sex hormone estrogen begins storing fat, and turns off the fat-burning hormones.

Then frustration and fear are released through dieting, skipping meals, and poor eating habits, contributing to the majority of fat gain. Fat has a mind of its own, and its purpose is to ensure your survival, not make you frustrated and fearful. It is, then, the reactions to these feelings, like poor eating habits, that encourage more storage of fat.

Even though with great conviction you want to lose fat specifically from your hips or thighs, the truth is that spot reducing is ineffective because when you lose fat it comes form a pool of fats (fatty acids) throughout your body, not from your one desired area. Yes, you can tone your muscles, but not your fat! Just like muscle can't turn into fat, neither can fat turn into muscle. It is when a physically active person stops exercising that muscles get smaller and smaller, decreasing the ability to burn fat. If they're still eating the same amounts of calories they'll naturally gain fat.

If you're overfat and on a very low-calorie diet with no exercise, you won't do as well as a friend who is dieting but exercising regularly and is protecting and building muscle while losing fat. If you are sitting around not exercising and restricting food, you are actually lowering your metabolic rate, causing you to burn fewer calories. Exercising speeds up your metabolic rate as more calories are burned. As muscle is destroyed it is replaced with fat, as your ability to burn calories keeps decreasing. To lose fat without exercising you have to literally starve yourself.

Excess fat stored in the body forms peroxides (rancid fats), resulting in illness. This happens because peroxides are damaging to the immune system, which consists of specialized cells, the spleen, bone marrow, and antibodies. There is a important substance that is part of the fat-burning process which is called L-carnitine.

L-carnitine is not a vitamin but an amino acid (protein). It can be made in small amounts by your body from lysine and methionine—two amino acids—and is also found in many foods.

A person who is a strict vegetarian or has a poorly balanced diet may have an L-carnitine deficiency, showing symptoms of elevated blood triglycerides or a renal disorder. L-carnitine is an amino acid material which transfers long-chain fatty acids across the membrane of the mitochondria within each cell, so they can be burned for energy and not stored as fat. As you can see, L-carnitine is necessary in fat metabolism because without it the body *can't burn fat*. L-carnitine is synthesized in the liver and kidneys and is then transported through the blood to the heart muscles and skeletal system, and accumulates in the muscle cells. If there isn't enough L-carnitine within the cells, the fatty acids are poorly metabolized and build up within the cells, leading to elevated blood fats.

L-carnitine can boost energy, along with decreasing fat and preventing the danger of ketosis, while getting rid of the bad breath and fatigue. We discussed earlier how the accumulation of ketone bodies in the blood causes it to become too acid, creating a loss of calcium, potassium, and many other nutrients.

Some foods that have a good amount of L-carnitine are chicken, milk, wheat germ, whole wheat bread, cauliflower, peanuts, and supplements sold in health food stores. There has been no U.S. Recommended Daily Allowance (RDA) established for L-carnitine, and the supplement's average per capsule is 250 milligrams. Always follow the instructions on the label and eat good healthy foods so your body has the energy to use the L-carnitine.

What is that lumpy, ripply-looking fat found on the hips, thighs and buttocks? Do the special rubber suits that make you look like part of a Star Trek episode, or the creams, hormone shots, massages, whirlpool baths, and vibrators help? Save your money, and start eating well, because cellulite can't be eliminated by any of the above techniques. I'm sure Captain Kirk would agree that cellulite is nothing but fat and poor skin and muscle tone. The rippled texture occurs because the skin will take on the shape of the fat underneath. This is why even a thin person can have cellulite. Losing fat too quickly and lack of exercise can cause the skin to lose its elasticity, resulting in saggy skin! Research has found that the fall and rise in blood sugar, and the hormone estrogen, which retains fluids, both slow down the elimination of waste. Both could contribute to cellulite formation. So eat the eat smaller, more frequent meals and get enough fiber in your eating program to keep you eliminating! Well, since we're already talking about the elimination process let's continue on and talk about digestion.

DIGESTION: YOU ARE WHAT YOU ABSORB

For you to understand the importance of foods and the dangers of food restricting, binging, or purging, you must understand digestion. You don't just swallow food and then take a starch blocker and hope you won't absorb those calories. Food is not simply absorbed directly into the bloodstream until it is broken down from large food molecules to smaller ones. For example, the carbohydrate part of a cookie is absorbed so quickly that the carbohydrate has been taken up and utilized by the time the food reaches the middle part of the small intestine.

Digestion is like a big blender, constantly in motion, and types of food vary as to how fast they will be absorbed, which is the reason not all calories are equal. Simple carbohydrates (sugars) are absorbed much more quickly, and as soon as they reach the small intestine they break down into smaller molecules such as glucose, and zap—they're in your bloodstream!

Unrefined whole complex carbohydrates, which contain fiber, are absorbed more slowly into the bloodstream, and the fiber component doesn't go into the bloodstream.

Digestion starts when you say, "Mmmm, that smells good!" This happens because your stomach is under neural and hormonal control, and the mere anticipation of food starts digestion. The smell stimulates the release of saliva in your mouth and gastric juices in your stomach. With each chew a piece of bread is being broken down by the digestives enzymes amylase or ptyalin as they begin the process of turning the bread into sugar. This is why you don't want to rush eating, because food needs to be chewed thoroughly so it can be masticated, making digestion and nutrient absorption more efficient.

Your stomach is about the size of your fist, and is like a collapsible elastic bag which lies in folds when it is not distended. When you eat you'll have distension of the stomach, and therefore distension of your belly. This is not fat, but healthy food; this is where food travels when you eat. I have meet hundreds of food restrictors who won't eat all week or the day before a special date so their stomach will be flat, and once they eat, they panic—thinking they are fat! Your stomach empties about 4 hours after a meal. You may have noticed that in the morning your stomach is flat. This is because food has moved out of the stomach and into the lower part of the digestive tract, and is ready to be eliminated.

When food is in your stomach, hydrochloric acid is secreted from the parietal cells of the stomach, along with gastric juices and intestinal enzymes, which begin liquefying the carbohydrates. The food is then passed along to the upper section of the small intestine (duodenum), which secretes pancreatic amylase.

The small intestine is where nutrient absorption occurs, and bile from the gallbladder is secreted to emulsify the fat and pancreatic lipase, and intestinal lipase splits fat molecules. Then the digested fat particles are absorbed through the intestinal walls.

The total breakdown of simple carbohydrates takes 15 minutes; complex carbohydrates take 1-2 hours depending on the fiber content. The more nutrients a food has, the slower the process, to ensure that more of the nutrients are being absorbed. This is why many dieters, especially severe food restrictors, get constipated when they eat. The body holds onto the food to absorb all the nutrients possible, in fear it may not get more food. Frying foods makes fats less digestible and destroys nutrients.

The saturated fats found in whole milk, yogurt, cheese, and beef, stay in the stomach longer, whereas the oils in fish and plants are primarily polyunsaturates and are digested more quickly. Nuts and seeds, which I suggested you eat as snacks, are rich in polyunsaturated fats like linoleic acid and oleic acid.

The digestive enzymes we have discussed are just a few of the enzymes that digest food and supply the body with the nutrients from food. Poor eating habits, binging, and purging all disrupt these enzymes and create digestive problems and poor health. Antacids act as a neutralizer buffer that provides initial relief, but later produces more acids. If you are having digestive problems, you can buy digestive enzyme capsules that contain pancreatin amylase, protease (trypsin and chymotrypsin), lipase, betaine HCL (betaine hydrochloride), pepsin, ox bile, bromelaine (from pineapple), and papain (from papaya). Follow the directions on the bottle, and if your digestive problem continues, see your doctor for further advice. It's better to be safe than sorry!

The starch blockers I mentioned earlier are dangerous because they alter starch digestion using oral amylase inhibitor, a substance which is supposed to prevent the absorption of starch calories. It is not effective in limiting the absorption of starch calories, but inhibited protein and other nutrients from digesting, causing flatulence and digestive disorders.

Another important substance needed to maintain a healthy digestive tract, especially if you've been purging, is acidophilus. Acidophilus is a healthy protective bacteria that keeps your intestines clean and eliminates constipation. Acidophilus is found in yogurt and other cultured products, which have many beneficial bacteria, such as *Bacillus bulgaricus* and *Lactobacillus acidophilus,* that hinder the growth of pathogenic organisms, protect against fungal and bacterial infections, and improve digestion and general health. You must keep a healthy intestinal flora so vitamins can be synthesized in your intestinal tract, like vitamin K, and the B vitamins—niacin, biotin, B_2, riboflavin, and folic acid. Acidophilus can be purchased at health food stores. Again, follow the directions on the bottle, and if a problem persists, see your doctor.

8

Conquering Your Sweet Tooth

It's Saturday afternoon and there is no food around except a few crumbs that happen to fall on the floor during the week, so off you go to the store. You're hungry—everything looks great! In the first aisle there are samples of a new fat-free sausage and it smells so good, but you hate sausage. You can feel yourself getting weaker and hungrier as you pass a person who has already started eating from their cart. Of course the next aisle is the cookies—two packs for the price of one. What a deal! Immediately you recall the possibility of having guests over in the next several months, and just can't pass up such a good deal!

In the car you go, and you can swear that there is someone talking to you—it's the cookies! "No," you promise yourself, yet a little voice sympathetically informs you on how well you've been dieting, so you carefully open a tiny corner of the package and gently slide one out, not disturbing the organization of the row. Mmmm ... that was good ... one more, no one will notice. Six blocks from home and an entire row has disappeared, and guilt and disappointment overwhelm you enough to eat the remaining row. You couldn't throw it away because that's wasteful, and you couldn't take it home because everyone knows you're on a diet, so you *had* to eat them. Didn't you?

That little sympathetic voice is back, saying, "What is wrong with me? Why can't I stay away from sweets, or eat just one? I'm such a sweet tooth." Why is it that two cookies or one donut isn't enough? You need more! Well, you're not crazy or alone, and you *can* do something to control it, by understanding the kinds of sugars found in foods, because there are good-tasting foods that can satisfy your sweet tooth.

There is the simple carbohydrate called sucrose, or table sugar. There is nothing wrong with sucrose when you eat it in moderation. For instance, the contents of foods are listed in descending order by weight, and the percentage of sugar doesn't have to be listed. However, if sugar is the first or second ingredient, guess what it contains the most of? Yes—sugar!

Choose wisely what you so quickly place into you mouth. Most natural sugars can be identified by their -ose ending, like galactose, lactose (milk sugar), sucrose (table sugar), and fructose or levulose (fruit sugar). Fructose and levulose are considered to be sweeter than sucrose, so you can use less of fructose but still get the sweetness desired, while consuming fewer calories. Fructose and levulose are believed to be absorbed more slowly than sucrose (table sugar), not causing an immediate rise and fall in blood sugar, and giving you more control. This is because fructose is absorbed by a slower process, called facilitated diffusion, not by active transport, like sucrose.

There are other sugars, such as sorbitol (found in chewing gum), mannitol, maltitol, and xylitol, which are sugar alcohols. These occur naturally in fruits, but can also be commercially produced. Brown sugar is nothing but white sugar with molasses syrup or caramel coloring added. Turbinado sugar is nothing but white sugar that has not gone through one of the refining processes, and there is nothing wrong with these sugars if you eat them in moderation and are not diabetic, or hypoglycemic.

There is so much controversy about honey versus table sugar, yet I believe that very few people overeat on honey. A teaspoon of honey has more calories than a teaspoon of sugar because it weighs more. Honey, however, is sweeter, so you need to use less than a teaspoon to get the sweetness you desire, and it does have some good nutrients, whereas sucrose (table sugar) has none.

Did you know there are many different kinds of honey? The next time you buy honey, look at all the different flowers they can come from which give them different textures, colors, and aromas. There are two types of honey: those made from one flower (unifloral honey) and those originating from several flowers (multifloral honey). For cooking, the lighter or milder honey is best because it doesn't disguise other flavors. Acacia is a mild honey and hardly every crystallizes, and clover is the next mildest. Lavender is a mild honey and is good in teas and on bread; it has a butterscotch taste. Dark, strong-tasting honeys are buckwheat, heather, and thyme. Orange blossom honey is more of a medium honey and has a good flavor. By eating more nutritious sweeteners, you can lose your sweet tooth.

Always buy pure unadulterated honey, and don't worry about it thickening or crystallizing; most honeys do. This is because of the sugar (glucose crystals) and pollen. Some honeys are more acid in their liquid state than in their solid state. When baking with honey, use it in liquid form. To change it from a solid to a liquid, don't boil it; just warm it slowly to preserve the nutrients and flavor. Try a little honey (lavender) on your popcorn, and roll some into ball. You can add some nuts and raisins, and eat in moderation.

What about artificial sweeteners like saccharin and cyclamate (marked under the name sucaryl) which contain no food value (no calories)? Sucaryl is a combination of ten parts cyclamate and one part Aspartame. Sounds appetizing, doesn't it? Saccharin is a by-product of petroleum, and I believe these artificial sweeteners worsen your sweet tooth. They are so much sweeter than the natural sugars we discussed, and therefore when eating natural sugars you need more in order to satisfy your sweetness level acquired from artificial sweeteners.

Aspartame, or NutraSweet, is an artificial sweetener that does contain calories just like regular sugar (four calories per gram). However, Aspartame is 180 times sweeter, so people are supposed to use less. Aspartame consists of two amino acids, L-Aspartic acid and L-Phenylalanine, and there is controversy and question over the safety of artificial sweeteners and their long-term effects. If you suffer from headaches, I suggest you stay away from artificial sweeteners. Even sorbitol, a natural sweetener, can cause gastrointestinal problems, including abdominal cramps and diarrhea, when 10 grams are consumed. Another sour note to this sweet story is that using artificial sweeteners has been linked to the raising of your set point. In other words, it may increase your storage of fat. Remember, there are no side effects to using moderation and self-control, which come from a better understanding of foods.

There are several natural sweeteners you may want to try, such as barley malt and bran rice syrup. These are carbohydrates present in the whole grain, and are called grain syrups. Grain syrups are produced when natural enzymes convert the starch in the grain to sugar, which the body metabolizes more slowly, keeping you in control. These sweeteners are easy to bake with and have a flavor that is more delicate than molasses and honey.

A couple of other sweeteners to use instead of artificial sweeteners are Eden Apple Butter or a pure fruit spread by Whole Earth, made with pear and apple.

Don't forget about moderation when eating any foods. Eating too many simple carbohydrates or refined carbohydrates can lead to a B vitamin deficiency. If you like ice cream, try Ice Bean (Farm Foods). It is comparable to ice cream and has less sugar and saturated fat. It tastes good, and gets better as you reduce the artificial sweeteners in your life.

Beware and read your labels when buying non-dairy frozen desserts (Tofu or soy milk). Most of them are good and honest in their labeling, containing about 25% fewer calories, no cholesterol, and no lactose or animal products. Some products are labeled tofu but use soy protein isolates. Ice Bean has water, soybean, and honey. The product Rice Dream is also good. If you like frozen fruit bars, make sure they are 100% pure fruit juice, not fruit punch, fruit drink, or fruit cocktail. Yogurt and frozen yogurt can have eggs and sugar added. A good yogurt with an honest label is Brown Cow Farm, which also has a Soygurt that tastes good!

Most granola bars and carob candy bars have more fat and sugar than a commercial candy bar. Carob candy bars use carob powder instead of chocolate, and honey instead of table sugar. They may have less fat and caffeine—that is, if it's an honest product. Most carob candy bars have palm kernel oil added to the carob powder to turn it into carob coating and end up with the same amount of fat as a commercial candy bar.

If you find yourself craving sweets, satisfying the craving all the time may be worsening the addiction, or sweet tooth. A few things you can do are to eat smaller, more frequent meals to keep your blood sugar stable, and don't eat highly sugared foods every day, but first every other day, and then work toward reducing it to twice a week. Cold turkey is not a good idea unless you don't mind feeling like you're insane! First, strengthen your immune system by slowly withdrawing sugar intake. Replace the sugars with complex carbohydrates high in fiber, which we'll talk about next. Start taking a vitamin and mineral supplement that contains calcium and chromium. That will help significantly. Watch what you eat, but above all watch what you think! If you are spending money on supplements and eating correctly but don't believe you can do it, you're defeating your purpose. You *will* do it, and feel stronger and healthier each day.

SAY YES TO FIBER!

Complex carbohydrates have been given a bad rap! Complex carbohydrates are whole grains, fruits, and vegetables. They are a good source of B vitamins, iron, and Vitamins A and C, and have a wonderful component called fiber. Fiber slows the rate of absorption of sugar over a longer period of time, reducing your craving for more sugar. The cereal 100% Bran has 2.5 grams of fiber per ounce, All Bran 2.3 has grams per ounce, Raisin Bran 1 gram per ounce, Shredded Wheat 0.85 grams per ounce, Wheaties 0.53 grams per ounce, Grapenuts 0.48 grams per ounce, and Total 0.52 grams per ounce. Fiber is the part of the plant cells that can't be digested by our enzymes or digestive secretions. Fiber helps your gastrointestinal system function smoothly. Fiber is not a laxative. It is an internal regulator that accelerates the transit time of food through the system, while absorbing liquid and producing bulk and a feeling of fullness. There is less strain to move your bowel and less risk of hemorrhoids and diverticular disease. If you are getting enough fiber your feces should be a medium to light brown and float.

This increase in transit time of fiber also decreases the risk of colon cancer by not allowing enough time for food to interact with unfriendly intestinal bacteria.

Fats will bind with fiber and move it through the system, resulting in fewer calories being absorbed. So have a salad before your main course and absorb fewer calories. This doesn't mean all you eat is fiber, and if you do, you won't like the side effect and neither will you friends. That's right—gas, or flatulence. Overloading your body with too much fiber causes the bacteria to ferment the fiber, causing flatulence, and can interfere with the absorption of calcium, as fiber binds to this nutrient, carrying it out of the body in your waste product.

Some complex carbohydrates, like beans, have two nonabsorbable carbohydrates, raffinose and stachyose, that are readily fermented by bacteria in the digestive tract. Soybeans are flatulence producers, but soybean products—like tofu or tempeh—are not, because they have had their carbohydrates broken down during processing. Cabbage, spinach, broccoli, brussels sprouts, and eggplant are gas-producing. Cellulose, pectin, and lignin are all forms of fiber. The highest amount of cellulose is found in bran, unpeeled apples, pears, peaches, and carrots. Pectin is found mostly in apples, grapes, carrots, and potatoes, and has gel-forming properties used to make jelly. Lignin (woody texture) is found in asparagus, sweet potatoes, peas, and whole grain breads, and can't be broken down or softened by cooking. Two other fibers found in most foods are hemicellulose and mucilages. All of these complex carbohydrates we discussed have a mixture of all these fibers but may have a little more of one than another. All these fibers help you control your sweet tooth by stabilizing your blood sugar.

These are all good healthy fiber nutrients. Some other excellent sources of fiber are radishes, lettuce, winter squash, celery, okra, green peppers, tomatoes, kidney and lima beans, all berry fruits (strawberries, raspberries, blueberries), and figs. Eat only fresh whole foods, not the canned ones, which have much less fiber.

Grains like millet, brown rice, buckwheat, quinoa (keen-wa), amaranth, oat bran, and oatmeal are good sources of fiber. Millet is one of the most complete proteins of all the grains. Millet, as well as amaranth and quinoa are good-tasting and can be used as a rice replacement. Try something new!

A few good cereals that you may not have tried are Kölln Fiber Cereals like Fruit Oat Bran Crunch and many more. If you would like some recipes, write to: Recipes Ko Information, c/o Edward and Son Trading Co., P.O. Box 3150, Union, NJ 07083. Another good cereal is Perky's Crispy Brown Rice, and Mother's Oat Bran Cereal. Seeds and nuts are good sources of fiber that can be added to cereals to increase their fiber, protein, and all-around nutrient value.

These foods also have high water content, which makes them low in calories. Fruits and vegetables are about 90% water, and bread is about 35% water, and even when fats and carbohydrates are broken down in the body they all produce what is called *metabolic water*. Therefore, the notion that drinking water with your meal dilutes and weakens your digestive enzymes is untrue, since water is found in all these foods and is also produced by their breakdown. Drink as much water as you like.

9

I'm Too Fat:
What Should I Eat?

You're feeling fat and nervous, especially when your stomach is filled with food, and the laxatives are so convenient. However, you've been wondering lately just how well they really work. Using laxatives to lose physical weight doesn't work. You're wasting your money and wasting valuable nutrients. This is because laxatives *do not* reduce calorie absorption. Laxatives do their work in the large intestine, and calorie and most nutrient absorption has already occurred in the small intestine. This same idea applies to purging. Your body has grown used to your purging, and has become skilled at absorbing calories and nutrients before you can purge them.

The empty feeling you experience from purging and laxative abuse and the reduction of physical weight seen on the scale are from dehydration—not fat loss. As soon as you stop using laxatives and purging, your body will rehydrate itself and you'll feel your tissues swelling with water as your body tries to regain its health. You, however, may think this swelling is fat, and panic and start using the laxatives again. Hang in there. In 5 to 25 days, your body will balance itself again. Every time you use laxatives or purge, you are losing valuable nutrients and disturbing your electrolyte balance. Electrolytes are minerals that become electrically charged when dissolved in your body's fluids. This electrical charge enables them to assist in the transmission of nerve impulses, muscle contractions, and body fluids, and in maintaining an acid-base balance. Taking laxatives and purging can cause malfunctioning of the heart, which is a muscle, and extreme fatigue and confusion, fainting, nausea, and many more complications. Put an end to laxative use and purging right now, and follow some of my next suggestions, taking it slowly, and a step at a time.

To begin, relax and remember that the swelling that is making you uncomfortable is not fat, but water gain. Your body is trying to replace the lost fluid from purging and laxative use. Stay off the scale because it only terrifies you. Give the scale to someone or put it in the *trash*—before it trashes you! Reduce your purging and laxative use slowly. Don't just go off of all your laxatives at once. Go slowly and then replace them with complex carbohydrates that have a good amount of fiber. Start taking a vitamin and mineral supplement to replace the nutrients lost, and digestive enzymes. Eat smaller, more frequent meals and don't overload your system because you'll fall back to the feeling that you need the laxatives and need to purge to get rid of your discomfort. You don't need laxatives or purging. They have just become familiar habits.

Another helpful nutrient that can help end purging is chlorophyll. Chlorophyll is a green pigment found in plants and other photosynthetic organisms. Chlorophyll can be purchased in the health food store in a liquid form that has a mint flavor to it. Nature's Way has a good product. You can use it as a mouthwash because the chlorophyll eliminates destructive strains of bacteria in the saliva, and helps lower the acid content of the mouth. Purging brings up many of the acids from the stomach and attacks the surface of the teeth, causing plaque, discolored teeth, and bad breath. Keeping your mouth clean and fresh will be a positive reminder of how good it feels to keep your body healthy and clean. Liquid chlorophyll helps get rid of the bad breath that comes from the formation of ketones during fat burning.

You know how you've been saying you just can't save any money—yes you can. I want you to save the money from the times you would buy laxatives, and reward yourself with something that makes you happy and gives you hope. Or give some of it to a charity and extend that hope to someone else! When everything is lost, you can still have *hope!*

BECOMING PROTEIN WISE

When people think of protein they usually think of a thick steak, a "stick-to-your-ribs" kind of food! Protein is important for everyone, not just the athlete or very active person. Even a couch potato whose sole exercise is changing the channel with the remote control needs protein. The Recommended Daily Allowance (RDA) is 60 grams of protein daily from both animal and plant sources. Depending on your body weight, age, stress level, general health, growth, pregnancy, lactation, and activity levels, the amount of protein needed can vary. The Food and Nutrition Board of the National Research Council suggests that a vegetarian needs more protein than a person who eats animal products.

Adults who eat animal meats and animal by-products need 0.9 grams of protein daily for every kilogram (2.2 pounds) of body weight. To calculate your protein need, divide your body weight by 2.2 and then multiply by 0.9. If you are a vegetarian, the Food and Nutrition Board suggests you multiply by 1.5.

Protein is the second most abundant body substance next to water. Protein is found in every cell in your body—hair, skin, nails, nerves, blood—and is important to building the hormone insulin and thousands of enzymes and antibodies that fight disease. Amino acids are the building blocks of protein. They contain nitrogen, which makes protein different from a carbohydrate or fat. Amino acids can be found in all protein foods in different combinations. Amino acids are found in collagen, a material that holds individual cells together and forms the contractile fibers that enable you to move.

The athlete or person on a high-protein diet may find that consuming more carbohydrates rather than more protein can increase endurance and stamina much more.   Carbohydrates have a protein-sparing effect. Too much protein for the athlete can actually decrease strength, because of the loss of water from the muscles, destroying them, as well as straining the kidneys and liver.

This destruction of muscles will lower metabolism (burn less calories). This is why protein diets to lose weight can actually make you fatter by lowering your metabolism through muscle loss.

If you consume more protein than you need, your body will have to get rid of the nitrogen-containing waste product of protein metabolism called urea. Urea is formed in the liver and excreted via the kidneys, and stresses both organs. The loss of water, which can lead to dehydration, is the way the body filters out the urea from the bloodstream. As you can see, high-protein diets are dangerous, and can cause dehydration and loss of many valuable minerals. What you see on the scale is *water loss*—not fat loss! Your doctor can give you a biochemical test that measures nitrogen balance, or the amount of urea in your blood plasma.

The loss of protein occurs during times of profuse sweating, blood destruction, injury, and psychological and physical stress. Protein is replaced constantly. Within a 6-month period, all the protein molecules break down (catabolism) and are rebuilt (anabolism) from new and recycled amino acids. Proteins are broken down in the body by digestion to amino acids and absorbed into the blood. Remember, don't use protein for energy, but carbohydrates and fats, so protein can be used as building material for cellular growth, repair, and maintenance. As I mentioned earlier, protein isn't stored in the body, and if not used for building material it is converted by the liver to a carbohydrate (gluconeogenesis) or to a fat (ketogenesis) and stored.

There are 23 amino acids, all of which your body needs, that can be combined together in a variety of ways to form protein. There are 8 out of these 23 amino acids that can't be manufactured in the body. They are called the 8 essential amino acids, and you must get them from the foods you eat. They are lysine, tryptophan, phenylalanine, methionine, threonine, leucine, valine, and isoleucine. A ninth—histidine—is essential for children. The rest are nonessential and can be manufactured by the body. Animal meat and animal by-products contain all the 8 essential amino acids in the correct proportion, as well as some nonessential amino acids. Plant proteins have some of the 8 essential amino acid but not all of them, and not in the correct proportion.

Eggs are the only non-meat food that contains the 8 essential amino acids in the ideal mixture, making them a complete protein. Nuts, grains, and seeds are lower in lysine and high in tryptophan, making them an incomplete protein. Legumes (peas, beans, lentils, nuts, and soybeans) contain a better amount of protein, are low in the amino acids cystine and tryptophan, but high in lysine, isoleucine, and methionine. However, grains and corn have good amounts of methionine and cystine and complement legumes. Soybean in the form of tofu is a complete protein. Tofu is processed similarly to cheese, and is almost equal in protein to fish. If you add rice to tofu you have a well balanced mixture of amino acids. By doing this, you are combining proteins from different sources to make what you are eating a more well balanced mixture of amino acids. This is referred to as *complementary proteins.*

A few more complementary proteins are: macaroni and cheese; cheese sandwich on whole wheat bread; peanut and almond butter; tahini (sesame seed spread) on whole wheat bread and a glass of low fat milk or soy milk. milk and cereal; beans and rice; lentil or split pea soup, potatoes and rice; and corn and peas. Try baking a potato and then add some low-fat cottage cheese or yogurt, spices, and broccoli to make it complete. Tempeh is a special food for vegetarians. It is a soybean cake that is a good protein without the fat and has B_{12} added. When you bake, try using soybean flour along with your whole wheat flour. It will give you a softer product with more protein. Keep an open mind and try some new foods!

If you're a strict "vegan," eating only food from plant sources, you may not be getting enough vitamin B_{12} and iron. For the vegetarian, only a few types of algae contain vitamin B_{12}. The iron that is found in plant sources is less absorbable because it is a non-heme iron. An alternative to animal meat and animal by-products is to eat meat analogs and fortified cereals where vitamin B_{12} and iron have been added, or take a vitamin and mineral supplement.

Some complete proteins are chicken, turkey, duck, pork, veal, lamb, beef, fish, yogurt, cheeses (including cottage cheese), milk, and eggs. If you need assistance, go to a health food store and ask someone to show you a few meat analogs, and you'll be surprised at how good they taste, and they don't leave you with such a full feeling, as animal protein can.

Keeping in mind that the RDA for protein is 60 grams, here are some amounts of protein found in different foods. Peanut butter has about 10 grams of protein in 1 tablespoon, most beans have 7-8 grams of protein per ½ cup, split pea and lentil soup 10 grams per ½ cup, one baked potato 3 grams, and most vegetables 1-2 grams per ½ cup. For every 1 piece of fruit there are 1-2 grams of protein. Grapefruit or orange juice is 2 grams per cup, wheat bread has 3 grams per slice and white bread 2 grams, most cereals range 4-6 grams, and most noodles, per cup, have 7 grams of protein. If you eat spaghetti with meatballs made of ground turkey you are consuming 19 grams of protein per cup. All milks, even skimmed milk, have 9 grams of protein per cup, cheeses per ounce range 5-7 grams, yogurt per cup is 8 grams. One egg is 6 grams, and most other meats, including fish, have 8 grams of protein per ounce. This does not include luncheon meats and ham, which have 6 grams per ounce.

As you can see, getting enough protein in your diet is easy to do. Next let's clear up the confusion about eating meats.

MEAT: IT'S YOUR CHOICE

Deciding what meats to buy can be a confusing experience. There are so many shapes, sizes, colors, and prices to pick from.

When buying meats, the "grades" given to different types are determined by the Agriculture Marketing Service, a government agency established for this purpose. This grading is a voluntary decision of, and paid for by, the meat packers. If the packer chooses to use this grading, it must be performed by trained government officials who must abide by federal standards.

The grade U.S. Prime is a tender, well marbled meat meaning more fat is distributed in the lean tissue. U.S.

Choice is also a tender meat, but has a little less fat or marbling. The grading U.S. Good is even less tender, having very little fat, and U.S. Standard is very lean meat that lacks marbling. Lastly, the U.S. Commercial grade is usually used for canned food and luncheon meats. Whatever grade of meat you decide to eat is your choice!

The dark meat has more vitamin B_1 and B_2, but is sometimes harder to digest than white meat because it has more connective tissue. It is the connective tissue that binds the meat fibers together to form muscle and connects these muscles to each other and to the bones. There are two types of connective tissue: collagen and elastin. These are not softened by cooking. Fish has very little, if any, connective tissue, and doesn't need to be cooked long.

The more exercised part of the animal has more connective tissue and is less tender. On the other hand, the less exercised part has very little connective tissue and therefore requires less cooking time to be tender. This is why many animals are not allowed to be free running but are kept crowded together in cages. If you want to use leaner cuts of meat, you can use a tenderizer made from proteolytic enzymes, such as bromelin, found in pineapples, papain, found in papayas, fictin, found in figs, and actinidan, found in kiwi fruit. These are all natural enzymes found in fresh fruit.

This is the reason you can't use fresh fruits like pineapple in Jell-o. The enzymes will break down the protein bonds and not allow your Jell-o to gel. Monosodium glutamate (MSG) is not a tenderizer, but a flavor enhancer. It actually increases the nerve impulses that are responsible for the sensation of flavor. So if you "can't eat just one," check your label and you may find out why.

Is that bright red surface on meat blood? No. It is actually a pigment called myoglobin, and the more myoglobin meat has the darker red it is. Beef contains more myoglobin than pork, and myoglobin increases with the age of the animal. When meat is heated the myoglobin turns a greenish-brown color. When you buy meat it has a special wrapping on it (called oxymyoglobin) that allows oxygen to enter and keep the pigment bright red. The wrap you use at home doesn't allow oxygen to enter, and your meat turns a greenish-brown. Many people think the meat is bad and throw it away. It is actually still good but merely lacks oxygen.

It is similar to cutting your skin: the blood comes out red because of the oxygen, but as it is deprived of oxygen and coagulates, it turns purple. I don't want you to get confused with the red color found in poor quality meat like, bacon, sausage, hot dogs, bologna, and salami. It is nitrite that makes these meats red. Otherwise they would be gray, which is not very appetizing, but then neither is nitrite. The nitrite is broken down into nitrous acid, which combines with hemoglobin in the meat to form the red color.

This is similar to what happens in your body as nitrite inactivates red blood cells and creates a condition called methemoglobinemia (inactivated hemoglobin). This condition causes extreme fatigue and irritability.

Children eat a lot of these foods. Make sure you find out what they are eating before you send them to their rooms. Nitrites are also known to combine in the stomach to form nitrosamines, which are cancer forming, and can cause allergic responses and hyperactivity.

Did you know there are over 2000 chemicals that are allowed in processing meats, all of which can be passed on to the consumer? If you are concerned by the antibiotics, tranquilizers, and growth-stimulating hormones used to slow down the animals' metabolism, making them fatter, or by the use of pesticides, there is something you can do! There are organic farms with clean surroundings that use no pesticides, hormones, or antibiotics, and that allow their animals to be free running. These meats can be purchased in health food stores.

Always cook your meat thoroughly. Poultry has chemicals just like beef, but birds live a shorter life than cattle and therefore the chemicals have less time to build up in their systems. Eating chicken, turkey, and fish is a much healthier idea; they are lower in saturated fat than beef, veal, pork, lamb, and even duck. Poultry is inspected and graded by trained government graders. The grading is also voluntary and is paid for by poultry processors. Grade A is of course the best, and grade B is less appealing in appearance and lacking in meatiness. The fat in fish actually has a class of polyunsaturated fats called Omega-3 fatty acids that lower blood cholesterol and raise HDL ("good cholesterol") even better than the polyunsaturated fats found in vegetables. The higher the fat content in fish, the better; it means they have more Omega-3 fatty acids.

Fish vary enormously in fat. Albacore, herring, salmon, mackerel, smelt, tuna, and shad are fatter fish. Leaner fish, with a fat content of less than 5% are halibut, flounder, haddock, perch, sole, and bass. Fish is highly perishable and should not be kept more than 10 days even if it is frozen. As soon as the fish dies the bacteria count continues to multiply, even when it is frozen, though at a slower rate. The frozen fish you buy could have been frozen for five years, because there are no standard regulations for fish. You are the inspector, so buy your fish fresh, not frozen. If fish is not frozen you can smell or feel the texture of the fish, making sure it is a mild smell and is firm to the touch. Don't eat fish raw; always cook it first.

Shellfish, like clams or oysters, should be tightly closed. If not, they have died and the bacteria is count is growing. Shellfish absorb pollutants from the water, such as inorganic mercury. Inorganic mercury converts into a highly toxic chemical called methyl mercury. As one goes up the food chain, with the larger fish eating the smaller ones, the mercury content increases. You may be getting more than protein from your fish. Eating mainly freshwater fish, rather than the larger salt-water fish, would be a safer idea.

DAIRY PRODUCTS: IT'S YOUR CHOICE

Whether you eat dairy products is really up to you. About a year ago I was standing in line at a grocery store and the woman in front of me was angry. She was telling the woman ahead of her, who was buying meat and animal by-products, that she was killing innocent animals. Yet she herself had a cart full of processed, adulterated, and refined foods, and I informed her she was a *people* killer! Strange how it's hard to see your own behavior.

Cheese, eggs, milk, and yogurt are good non-meat protein, and milk has about 9 grams per cup whether it's skim or whole. Milk has vitamins A, D, B_2, B_{12}, phosphorus, and traces of other nutrients. These nutrients in milk should be kept from the light. Years ago, boxes were used to prevent the detrimental effects of light (sunlight and fluorescent light). Low-fat and skim milk are more susceptible to light damage and nutrient loss than whole milk because they have fewer fat globules to disperse the light. Keep milk in its carton to prevent light penetration, so it will retain its nutrient value.

Some states allow Certified Raw Milk under controlled conditions.

Milk, however, is always pasteurized and homogenized. Pasteurized means that milk is heated to 62 degrees centigrade for 30 minutes, which reduces the number of bacteria. Unpasteurized milk can cause disease. Homogenizing milk disperses the fat throughout the milk so the fat doesn't rise to the top.

The skin that forms on cooked milk is similar to what forms on pudding, which is a protein called casein, and the substance that burns at the bottom is another protein called whey.

The precipitation of the protein casein found in milk is part of the process used to make cheese, yogurt, cottage cheese, sour cream, and buttermilk. Milk is cultured with bacteria that convert the lactose in the milk to lactic acid. Then the lactic acid produced by the bacteria causes the precipitation of casein in milk. When you make cream soups and add asparagus, the tannin in this vegetable can cause a similar kind of curdling. People whose digestive systems produce little or no lactase—an enzyme that digests lactose (milk sugar)—can have cultured milk, like sweet acidophilus milk, which is pasteurized and the bacteria *lactobacillus acidophilus* added. Buttermilk has the same amount of fat as nonfat milk except it is more acidic.

Whole milk contains 3.25% milk fat, and there are low-fat milks that contain 1%, 1.5%, 2%, or 2.5%. Skim milk must contain less than 0.5% milk fat. Vitamin A and D are add to skim and low-fat milk because they were taken out to make lower-fat milk. This happens because fat acts as a carrier for the fat-soluble vitamins A, D, E, and K, which are removed along with the fat.

A non-dairy alternative to milk is Eden Soy Milk, called Sunsoy. Yogurt is a great source of calcium, protein, and B vitamins and is comparable to milk cup for cup. The friendly bacteria in yogurt used in the fermentation process, like *L. bulgaricus* and *S. thermophilus* species, convert lactose to lactic acid. These friendly bacteria keep your intestinal flora healthy. Add your own fresh fruit to your yogurt and buy low-fat yogurt. Naja Acta Dane is a good yogurt you can find in grocery or health food stores.

Ever since the big cholesterol scare, cheese and eggs have been on the least-wanted list. Cheese, however, is another good food rich in protein, vitamins, and minerals. But it contains saturated fat and is so easy to eat a lot of, especially with crackers! Moderate amounts of part skimmed or low-fat mozzarella, swiss, ricotta, or low-fat cottage cheese, feta cheese, parmesan are good choices. The soft and semi-soft cheeses are higher in water and lower in fat. Cheddar, a hard cheese, is higher in fat in comparison to swiss and mozzarella. Cream cheese has the same amount of fat as butter. There is a terrific soy cheese called Soya Kaas, which comes in mozzarella and cheddar flavors and contains no cholesterol and very little fat, if any! It's great on tacos and whole wheat toast, casseroles, etc.

Unripened cheeses such as cottage cheese, ricotta, neufchatel, and mozzarella are more economical than ripened cheeses. Examples of ripened cheeses are limburger, brie, monterey jack, muenster, colby, cheddar, swiss, romano, and parmesan.

Processed cheese is dead food; it has had the life taken out of it and, ironically, it is more expensive than real cheese! Cheese food is processed cheese with low-fat dry milk added to it along with water. Next let's discuss oils.

OILS: RISKS AND BENEFITS

It certainly can be confusing deciding which is the best oil to use. There are several good reasons to prefer vegetable oils over animal fats.

A saturated fat is usually hard at room temperature, like butter, or fat in beef (except for coconut oil and palm oil, which are saturated but are liquids). Unsaturated fatty acids and polyunsaturates are liquid at room temperature, like safflower oil, olive oil, sesame seed oil, peanut oil, corn oil, and other oils from nuts, seeds, and vegetables. Vegetable oils contain the essential fatty acids linolenic, linoleic, and arachidonic, which can't be manufactured by your body and must be supplied by the food you eat.

These essential fatty acids are necessary for maintaining healthy skin, hair, blood, arteries, and nervous system. Some good food sources that contain these essential fatty acids are sunflower or pumpkin seeds, whole grains, beans, oatmeal, and a variety of soups like tomato and chicken soup. They are also available in smaller quantities in meats.

Margarines and vegetable shortenings, commercial peanut butter, palm oil, and some candies are made by a process called hydrogenation (hydrogen is added) to unsaturated oils, making them solid at room temperature. Hain's safflower oil margarine, or cashew, almond, or sesame seed butter are good to use in place of butter, applying in moderation, of course.

All foods—vegetable and animal—contain a mixture of saturated, monounsaturated, and polyunsaturated fatty acids. Animal fats are usually more saturated than vegetable oil. For example, butter is 4% polyunsaturated, 37% monosaturated, and 59% saturated, compared to safflower oil, which is 78% polyunsaturated, 12% monounsaturated, and only 10% unsaturated. Safflower oil is one of the highest of all the vegetable oils in the essential fatty acids (linoleic). Vegetable oil is better than butter. Yet it is still 100% fat and can cause an increase in blood triglycerides. Among animal fats, beef has a higher percentage of fatty acids than poultry or fish.

Other oils that contain more polyunsaturated fats are soybean oil (63%), cottonseed oil (59%), corn oil (58%), and olive oil (4polyunsaturated, 81% monounsaturated, and 12% unsaturated). Peanut oil is 31% polyunsaturated, 46% monounsaturated and 23% saturated. Coconut oil is 0% polyunsaturated, 8% monounsaturated, and a big 92% saturated. Coconut oil is found in many granola cereals and granola bars, candy bars, and many other foods. Both polyunsaturated and saturated fats increase our body's need for vitamin E, and most oils have vitamin E added as a preservative or antioxidant to prevent the oil from going rancid. Frying foods and overheating, burning, or reusing oil is not a healthy idea. It causes the glycerin in the fat to be changed into acrolein, which causes flatulence and heartburn. Overcooking foods, especially meats, makes fat less digestible.

How do you know what is the best oil to buy? Many oils are extracted using the hexane process. Hexane is the most common chemical used in solvent extraction. This is a highly volatile, toxic petroleum derivative, and at the end of the process some of this solvent residue remains in the oil. Then the oil is heated at high temperatures to evaporate the toxic solvent, but there are nutrients and flavor that also are lost.

Oils such as peanut, sesame, and sunflower only need low heat and low pressure to yield oil. The only oil that can be labeled cold pressed is olive oil, and make sure the oil you select is labeled expeller-pressed and unrefined. These oils taste much more flavorful and are more nutrient-rich. Keep your oils refrigerated; the more unsaturated the oil the faster it will become rancid and burn more easily. Safflower oil doesn't have much of a flavor, and soybean oil has a strong taste and is good for stir frying. Olive oil and peanut oil are good on salads, and sesame seed oil can be used all different ways and tastes quite good.

CHOLESTEROL

Big bad cholesterol. It's not so bad. As a matter of fact, you couldn't survive without it. Cholesterol is not a fat, but a wax or sterol. Your liver and intestine synthesize cholesterol from saturated fat, and there are 20 different enzymes needed for this process. Cholesterol is also manufactured from the breakdown of carbohydrates and protein. The RDA for cholesterol is 300 milligrams. One egg provides around 250 milligrams, almost meeting the RDA.

The sex glands and the adrenal gland use cholesterol to make specific hormones. For example, the female sex hormone estrogen decreases cholesterol. It's your liver that converts cholesterol into the bile required for proper food digestion (specifically, for fat emulsification). Cholesterol is found in animal products, not fruits, vegetables, nuts, or grains. Eating carrots and many other vegetable fibers can help reduce cholesterol. It is the calcium pectate present in the carrot fiber that represses bile acid production used in digestion, forcing the body to draw down its cholesterol to produce more of the bile acids. This is one reason why garlic is so famous for reducing cholesterol, as well as onions.

The American Heart Association states that the average total plasma cholesterol level of 180-200 mg/dl (milligrams of cholesterol per deciliter of blood) in the adult population indicates a low risk of cardiovascular disease. Although total cholesterol is an important indicator of risk, an even more precise measurement is the LDL cholesterol level.

You may have heard the terminology HDL (High Density Lipoproteins) and LDL (Low Density Lipoproteins). The LDLs (bad cholesterol) transport cholesterol through the blood and deposits it in the arteries. HDLs (good cholesterol) do the opposite, taking cholesterol away from the lining of the arteries. This is why it is recommended to lower fat consumption—due to the increased levels of LDLs and serum cholesterol occurring in foods high in saturated fats like meats, butter, egg yolks, and even shrimp, lobster, and oysters. So eat these foods in moderation. Moderation equates with *good health.*

You want to have low levels of total cholesterol, LDL cholesterol, VLDL (Very Low Density Lipoprotein) cholesterol, and triglycerides (blood fats) as well as a low cholesterol ratio, while keeping a high level of good, protective HDL. Have your cholesterol checked at your doctor's office and they'll take a blood sample. Before the test, you must fast for 12-14 hours before blood is drawn.

BECOMING FOOD WISE

I want you to become food wise, not food restrictive. Have you ever read a label and said "What is that stuff?" Start asking yourself, "How can that food sit on the shelf for three years and not spoil?" What is artificial chocolate flavoring?—yuk! Most of the popular soft drinks are high in sugar, sodium, and phosphorus, and have a long shelf life. It is the phosphoric acid that is added to hold the sugar in suspension so it will not crystallize that gives it a long shelf life. There is nothing wrong with phosphoric acid, sodium, or sugar in soft drinks consumed in moderation. Pop is something most people overuse, especially if it says, "only one calorie." Too much pop can cause loss of calcium from the body. Even meats, chocolate, and caffeine contain phosphoric acid and cause depletion of calcium stores. Too much sugar also causes calcium losses.

Becoming a label reader is another way to take care of your body.

As you begin to introduce new foods into your eating plan, read labels on the foods you purchase, or you're getting ripped off! When you're not food wise, you're being robbed of nutrients, your health, and your money! Buy foods that don't have a long list of ingredients, such as fresh fruits and vegetables. There is no list of ingredients that comes on an apple or a carrot stick! Eat whole natural fresh foods that spoil! Stay away from processed, refined, adulterated (addition of chemicals) foods that are also higher in calories and low in nutrients. These types of foods are missing what is needed for the metabolism of food in the body and brain, and sit in your stomach for a longer period of time until your body can figure out how to get rid of them!

These types of foods are usually more expensive, not because they are healthier for you, but because the storage and processing to keep them from spoiling are costly. Bread, for example, starts out as a highly nutritious food until it is refined and the bran and wheat germ are taken out. All that is left is the endosperm (starch) and a more expensive bread because of the process. It is also bleached to look a pretty white color. When bread is refined, it loses 22 nutrients; through an enrichment process, only three B vitamins, vitamin D, calcium, and iron are replaced. I hardly call this a fair exchange of nutrients!

Items are not always what they appear on the label, and all substances in a food product don't have to be listed on the label, which can be misleading. A food that states "no salt" could still have sodium. The word "light" could be referring to the color and not its caloric content, and if you don't read the label you'll fall hook, line, and sinker! The words "sugar free" don't mean it is lower in calories; it may still have artificial or non-nutritive sweetener added.

Another example of how misleading advertising can be is the labeling of fat content. It may sound good to you if you see hot dogs labeled as "95% fat free" (by weight). But you are not interested in how much the fat weighs. You want to know how many of the hot dogs' calories come from that fat. That would be about 50-80%, since fat has a lot more calories than do carbohydrates or protein. For food to be truly "low-fat," fat should not comprise more than 25% of the food's total *calories,* not its weight.

Let's say a label states that a food contains 550 calories per serving and 35 grams of fat per serving.

What does that tell you? Nothing—until you do a simple calculaiton to see if the food is more than 25% fat. Since fat has 9 calories per gram, multiply the number of grams of fat (also listed on the label) by 9. For example, if the product has 35 grams of fat, 9 × 35 = 315 calories of fat. Then divide the calories of fat (315) by the calories per serving (550). This gives you 0.57, which when multiplied by 100 to get a percentage equals 57%. Therefore 57% of that food's total calories come from fat, and it could not be classified, and should not be thought of, as a low-fat food.

All products labeled "low calorie," "reduced calorie," "diet" or "dietetic" fall under the FDA (Food and Drug Administration) and must contain no more than 40 calories or have a least one-third fewer calories than the regular product of that type. If a product is labeled "enriched" or "fortified" it means vitamins and minerals and/or protein have been added, and the product must have nutrients labeled. If the word "imitation" appears on the label, it means the product is nutritionally inferior to the real thing. The word "natural" doesn't mean anything, unless used on meats and poultry labeling, because the FDA has no regulations on the word "natural." I'm sure you are realizing why it is important to become food wise. Even the word "naturally flavored" holds no guarantee that artificial colors, additives, or preservatives have not been added. Just because it says "one calorie" doesn't make it a perfect food!

The USDA (United States Department of Agriculture) has no regulations on the word "organic." Labels indicating that the product is sugarless or sugar-free mean that it can't contain sucrose (table sugar), but it can contain other sweeteners, like fructose, honey, syrup, sorbitol, and mannitol.

Even mineral water has no regulation on it, and could be regular tap water with minerals added. Lastly, when buying bread, wheat bread is really the same as white bread. You want to buy *whole wheat* bread, and "whole wheat" should be the first ingredient listed. Take your time and make good choices for yourself. It's *your* body. Take a shopping list with you, so you don't get frustrated trying to remember everything and then just grab anything off the shelf! If you like to eat frozen dinners, which are usually nutritionally incomplete in calcium and B vitamins as well as fiber, add to the dinner a salad or some brown rice or whole wheat bread to increase the nutrient value. Once you start taking your time, you'll realize that the chunk tuna you've been buying is more expensive than the flaked tuna, or mackerel is less expensive than salmon or tuna.

10

Food Safety and Cooking Tips

I'm notorious for burning food, and if you tend to burn, and find your smoke alarm going off while you cook, it is best not to cook in dark surfaced pots or pans that absorb heat! Excessive heating or burning of any foods makes them difficult to digest. Try using stainless steel pans that reflect some of the heat, preventing excessive burning; even though you may have developed a taste for "dark crunchy food," it isn't healthy. Also, foods that are high in fats and sugars brown more readily, so be aware!

Let's discuss a few ways to save nutrients and prevent bacteria growth. You should always cook frozen food from the frozen state or thaw it in the refrigerator. Do not allow it to thaw at room temperature. Bacteria grow at room temperature and body temperature, but are destroyed when exposed to heat of 150°F (60°C) for about 30 minutes. Just because you refrigerate or freeze food doesn't mean it destroys bacteria. Freezing can only slow down or stop multiplication of bacteria until the food is returned to room temperature. If you want to reduce the chances of food poisoning, keep things refrigerated and cook them well. If you like chicken, cook it well, because 85-95% of chicken (before it is cooked) contains salmonella. If chicken needs to be thawed quickly, submerge it in *cold* water; thawing it at room temperature only invites bacterial growth.

Poultry and meats can be stored safely in plastic wrap for two days. When you reheat foods, heat them all the way through to at least 165°F. Veal, beef, and lamb should be heated to 140°F, poultry to 160°F and pork to 150°F. Pork should be cooked extremely well, because it contains larvae that causes trichinosis, a life-threatening disease.

Never forget to wash poultry, fish, pork, etc. Even vegetables and fruits may contain a worm that carries a disease. This is why it is important that all utensils, after cutting, be washed to prevent cross-contamination. If you're going to cook, take special care in what you do.

If you want to save nutrients, try steaming vegetables. When you boil them, the nutrients just end up in the water, not in your body. When making a salad you should rip, not cut, the lettuce, because cutting damages the enzymes, causing nutrient loss.

To clean your fruit and vegetables, try using a product called Fruit Wash. You spray and rinse your fruits and vegetables with it and it removes waxes, pesticides, and many other harmful chemicals.

Eggs contain *Salmonella,* as do uncooked beef, pork, poultry, and sometimes raw dairy products. *Salmonella enteritidis* can cause severe illness, abdominal pain, nausea, and diarrhea. Don't eat eggs that are cracked, or that have not been refrigerated, and don't put eggs in the egg holder, because every time you open and close the door the eggs change temperature. Keep your eggs in the carton and keep them refrigerated. Some cheap mayonnaise manufacturers may use cracked eggs, just like some bakeries may use cracked eggs, because they are much less expensive, and they need a lot of them, but it's best to avoid this practice.

Eating fresh whole foods will give you more taste and nutrients, making you feel more satisfied. Foods that are high in sugar and lack nutrients don't make you feel satisfied—and you keep on eating. Try using as few canned foods as possible. I refer to canned foods as dead foods. Try this experiment: Place one can of green beans on the kitchen counter and then take a fresh green bean and place them side by side for several days. (This could also be done with fresh or canned peaches.) You'll notice that the molecular structure of the canned green beans never changed its shape. It is dead food. The fresh green bean, however, will be wrinkled because its molecular structure has changed. It is a living food. If you do buy canned food, make sure the cans aren't dented or bulging; if they are, the food may contain botulinal toxins.

Acidic foods shouldn't be stored in cans after opening, especially tomatoes or fruit juices. It is the acid in the food that causes the lead from the can to bleed into the food. Many canned foods have a metallic taste, a taste I find undesirable. Buying fresh or frozen foods should always be your first choice. If you're going to buy fresh foods, learn how to store them to preserve freshness. Once you start eating fresh, whole foods that don't come with a list of ingredients, you'll "can the whole thought."

Irradiation of foods is another method of food preservation. Commercial food irradiation started in 1986, and the FDA has listed foods that are approved for irradiation, such as fruits and vegetables, and dry or dehydrated herb or vegetable seasonings. Irradiation destroys bacteria and insects in food, and prolongs the shelf life by slowing down the ripening of foods. Experiments have shown that no detectable traces of radioactivity remains, but I still remain skeptical. This process causes the destruction of many valuable nutrients as well as the taste and texture of foods, especially meats. More research needs to be done and the cost is still too high in comparison to other food treatment processes, so read your label!

THE MOST IMPORTANT NUTRIENT: WATER

Most people don't even think of water as being a nutrient. It is the water in your soft drink that quenches your thirst, and the sugar and salt that make you thirsty enough to keep on drinking more! Scientific testing has been done which proves that sugar does increase thirst. Consuming these drinks when exercising or before exercising can cause you to burn out sooner.

The sugar and salt act to draw vital water into the stomach and away from the part of the body that needs it the most—the muscles. You can only survive about 10 days without water. Water comprises about 75% of body weight for men and 65% for women. Men hold more water because they have more muscle, and muscle holds more water than fat.

Water doesn't serve just to quench thirst. It is also needed for the transport of oxygen, nutrients, and hormones, and functions as well to rid the body of waste products. Even the sounds you hear are transmitted by fluids in the inner ear.

Water is vital to the body, especially during times of exercise. You should drink water before, during, and after exercise. Don't forget to fuel up before you exercise with complex carbohydrates, like a piece of fruit or two slices of whole grain bread, which digest faster than fatty foods. Try eating about one hour before you exercise. Eating high-fat foods before exercising can slow you down, and sugar will lower blood glucose and cause fatigue later when you're ready to exercise.

Water doesn't interfere with the digestion of food, unless you've had part of your stomach removed. Drink plenty of water, whenever you want. Water helps your liver and kidneys function better. All foods contain their own water; even carbohydrates, protein, and fats consist of carbon, hydrogen, and oxygen, and when broken down all produce water called *metabolic water*. Even bread contains 36% water, and fruits and vegetables about 95%. Always drink water when you're thirsty and don't restrict drinking water simply because you want to weigh yourself after you exercise.

If you are concerned about the chemicals in water you can do several things. You can get a purifying system, let your water stand for three days to get rid of the chlorine, boil it for 1-2 hours, or use an activated charcoal filter. There is an inexpensive water filter system called Pure Crystal by BRITA that removes 90% of the chlorine, lead, copper, etc. It also prevents bacterial growth. You need to periodically buy a replacement filter, and it can be purchased at health food stores. Another option is buying bottled water, like purified water or spring water, which contains nutrients but no harmful chemicals. Distilled water has no nutrients and no harmful chemicals.

11

Shaping Up

Do you feel you're not fit enough to exercise? Most people who complain about not having enough energy are usually not getting any exercise.

I've met hundreds of people who are looking for that energy pill! Exercise doesn't mean you have to become another Mary Lou Retton! Exercise can mean walking the dog. Walking is a wonderful aerobic exercise that burns fat and uses 650 muscles while conditioning the heart. As muscle tissue increases, so does your ability to burn fat.

Exercising about 20-30 minutes three or four times a week will help you shape up and give you energy, not burn you out! It is much harder to get in shape than to maintain good shape, and initially it takes a lot of discipline and time, but it can be done. Getting back in touch with your body can give you an ultimate sense of freedom. Shaping up can be fun! Think of your body as a big clump of clay; through exercise you can mold it any way you wish!

GETTING STARTED

When you first begin exercising, start out slowly and then gradually increase your range of motion. For example, start walking 15 minutes three times a week. Make sure you have a variety of activities that will give your muscles a workout and, most important, eliminate boredom. Get smart, and vary your activities. Brisk walking, jump roping, cross country skiing, swimming, running, bike riding, aerobic dance—all these increase the body's use of oxygen. Non-impact and low-impact aerobics classes are the best for starting out; they have fewer jumping and jarring movements, and therefore there is less chance of injury. Non-impact aerobics is done in place, with arm movements combined with stepping to raise heart rate.

The word *aerobic* means "in the presence of oxygen," and it is your ability to use and transport oxygen which measures how fit you are. Aerobic activities are long-lasting rhythmic activities that promote an increase in heart rate above 120 beats per minute. (Each person must determine for themselves what heart rate is normal and safe for them, since heart rates vary among indviduals. Heart rate charts are guidelines, not absolutes. Always listen to your body, and to your doctor.) When exercising to lose fat, time is more important than intensity, and pain is a signal that something is wrong, not a threshold to be crossed. Don't confuse pain with discomfort. If you are weight lifting, rest after each set for 15 seconds and then do another set. All exercising should be controlled body movements—not jerking movement, but smooth and in control.

Other activities, like tennis, volleyball, and softball, are anaerobic activities and help to improve agility and coordination because the muscles are forced to react quickly. Swimming is an aerobic activity that improves the upper body strength. Walking does not unless you carry hand weights or wear wrist weights when you walk. Weightlifting and pushups aren't aerobic but get your heart pumping and build strength. Always warm up and cool down when you engage in any of these activities. Always drink a good amount of water to nourish your electrolytes, which are minerals that become electrically charged when dissolved in your body's fluids. These electrical charges enable them to assist in the transmission of nerve impulses, muscle contractions, and body fluids, and maintain acid-base balance.

OVEREXERCISING: PUSHING IT

Exercising can become a negative when you get upset about missing a day and fear your body will get fat, or muscle will atrophy. Overexercising is dangerous and counterproductive, because the more you push your body the more it fights back. Everyone needs some days off to rest, which is the time your body needs to make some positive changes, like increasing your strength, muscle mass, and ability to burn more fat.

Going to extremes and developing a very rigid routine has created an *overcontrol* in fear of losing control, similar to eating problems. I've seen many people move their overcontrol from eating onto exercising. Exercise should, as I mentioned earlier, give you a feeling of freedom, not restriction and fear. Exercise should not be a form of self-punishment done when you feel guilty about eating. Furthermore, if you are not eating well and lack important nutrients like calcium, your body is weaker and you become more susceptible to injury and illness. Moderate exercise is better and prompts the body to conserve carbohydrates by producing more of the enzyme that burns fat!

The key to exercising is not *over*exercising. It is best to engage in moderate levels of exercise but for a longer period of time, not high intensity for a short time. So the longer you exercise, the less the intensity has to be, and your body relies on your oxygen system (aerobic) for energy production, and you're burning fat. Your body uses separate pathways for metabolizing fats and sugars, depending on the intensity of the exercise.

If you're exercising and breathing becomes difficult, you're probably burning sugar, not fat. If breathing gets difficult, slow down slightly. High-intensity exercise bouts only burn you out fast and don't burn fat! Develop your own pace. If you are exercising with someone, listen to your body; don't try and keep up with your partner—just do your best!

Once exercise becomes too intense, the fats can't continue to be used as a major energy source and your body will begin to use carbohydrates (sugar) from the muscles and liver. Once your body gets in good shape it is easier to maintain, even with less exercise. This happens because fat will be replaced by firm muscle. You may notice an increase on the scale, which indicates weight gained in lean muscle mass, not fat. In other words, you may be "overweight" but not overfat, because muscle weighs more than fat! Some good news is that muscle may weigh more but it takes up one-fifth the space of fat, so you may weigh more but be inches smaller. So get rid of the scale.

Are you hungry after you exercise? It could be psychological, if you are well nourished. During exercise your appetite should be lower because there is a redirection of the blood flow from the digestive tract, stimulating the muscular use of blood fat instead of blood sugar. Raising body temperature through exercise also tends to lower appetite. You should feel good after exercising, and most people do. Even the person who has to be forced to exercise will admit how good they feel afterward! There is a biochemical reason for this. Endorphins, which are chemically present in the brain, can be activated by exercise, stress, and mental exercise, and they can kill pain and give you a feeling of well-being!

12

Vitamins and Minerals:
Do You Need Them?

Are people who take vitamin and mineral supplements "health nuts"? If so, I'm one of those "nuts." I believe we all need a vitamin and mineral supplement that reflects the RDA and is used as a kind of "natural band-aid" in conjunction with healthy eating. The RDAs are value judgments, and were initially set by the Food and Nutrition Board (FNB) of the National Research Council in 1943. They are reviewed about every five years, depending on current research findings and changes in living patterns. They are the levels that are recommended for daily consumption by healthy people.

If you are a chronic dieter who is consuming fewer than 1200 calories (for women; less than 1800 calories for men) you should seriously consider a vitamin and mineral supplement. But remember, just taking a vitamin and mineral supplement isn't going to keep you healthy if you're eating unhealthy foods or severely restricting food. This is because vitamins and minerals transform food into energy, and food is required for vitamins and minerals to perform their functions.

We all have different biological needs, and therefore I suggest a trip to the doctor's office for a blood chemistry profile, which will reflect your general health and nutritional needs. The fear about using a vitamin and mineral supplement is that people will engage in "armchair doctoring" and not seek professional diagnosis and treatment of what might be a serious illness. Vitamin and mineral supplements are not pills or medications; they are concentrated food substances usually extracted from plant or animal sources. A few examples are vitamin C, which comes from rose hips; vitamin A is usually extracted from fish liver oil; and vitamin E comes from wheat germ or soybean. Most B vitamins come from yeast or liver. Because vitamins and minerals are concentrated food sources, you can get 500 milligrams of vitamin C without having to eat a dozen oranges. If you wanted to meet the 18-milligram recommended daily allowance for iron, you would have to eat 3000 calories daily. If you're "dieting," this will be impossible to meet.

Let's discuss the difference between natural and synthetic vitamins. It does not matter whether the vitamin is natural or synthetic, because your body cannot differentiate between them, since their molecular structure is the same, and they are therefore used the same way in the body. You may have noticed vitamin supplements labeled "conatural," which means they're part synthetic and part natural. There is, however, a nutritional advantage to buying a natural vitamin, because it is more complex in nutrients. For example, synthetic vitamin C is only ascorbic acid, whereas natural vitamin C contains bioflavinoids—the whole C complex family found in nature. Natural vitamin E contains all the eight tocopherols, whereas synthetic vitamin E just contains alpha tocopherols, not beta, delta, etc.

When taking a vitamin and mineral supplement, use it in good judgment and in moderation; more is not necessarily better. Supplements should be taken with a meal. If not they will leave your body within two hours instead of four or five, allowing less time for the body to use them. Vitamins and minerals should be kept in dark, cool places with the cover closed tightly.

Let's discuss why moderation and care should be taken when using a vitamin and mineral supplement. The reason vitamin A, D, E, and K are called fat soluble is that they are stored in our fat, and can build up when too much is ingested, causing toxicity. This usually happens when people are trying to treat illness, thinking that taking more will be better. Supplements should be used as a means of prevention, promoting wellness, not treating illness. Just as food is necessary and good for you, but can be destructive to the body when consumed in excess (causing obesity), vitamins and minerals, which are concentrated food substances, can also be bad for you when used excessively.

Another point is that everyone has slightly different needs due to individual differences in height, weight, age, and physical activity. Find what works best for you.

If water-soluble vitamins and minerals like vitamin C and the B complex vitamins are taken in excess, they will be excreted. This occurs because when a vitamin enters the body it will travel through the bloodstream to a specific body cell, and then form part of the enzyme complex within the cell. The cell, however, has a limited ability to produce these enzymes, and once that capacity is reached the vitamins cannot be used. They will then be excreted in the urine, especially the water-soluble vitamins. The fat-soluble vitamins are likely to be stored, although they are still excreted to some extent in the feces and urine.

Bear in mind that vitamins and minerals function best when they work together, or *synergistically*. This is why taking a multi-vitamin and mineral supplement guarantees more of a scientifically well-balanced formula, in which the elements function together, enhancing one another's effectiveness in the body. For example, zinc, a mineral, is needed in order for vitamin A to be pulled from storage in the liver. Another example is calcium, which is absorbed better when taken with vitamins C and D and magnesium. Calcium and phosphorus, which are both minerals, function best in a 2:1 ratio. An imbalance can form in these minerals when too much meat, soft drinks, caffeine, and chocolate are ingested; they increase levels of phosphorus, creating an imbalance. Eventually, high levels of phosphorus can cause the depletion of calcium. The minerals calcium and magnesium also need to be in a unique ratio (2:1), and tea (tannic acid), coffee (caffeine), and antacids all interfere with calcium absorption. Eating foods high in sugar and protein increase the body's need for calcium and B_6.

Next I will discuss in detail some common vitamins and minerals and how they're important in keeping you healthy. When you're restricting food or binging and/or purging, you throw out of balance all these nutrients that allow you to think clearly, exercise, and be happy and healthy. Once you finish reading this section you'll think twice before you start on a restrictive "diet" of not eating and misery! Let's take a closer look at the wonderful nutrients found in foods.

A LITTLE ON MINERALS

There are 106 known elements and 92 occurring in nature. The minerals in your body fall into two classes: macrominerals, like calcium, phosphorus, magnesium, sodium, potassium, and chloride, which are present in the body in larger amounts, and trace minerals or microminerals, like iron, manganese, copper, iodine, zinc, fluoride, selenium, molybdenum, chromium, aluminum, boron, arsenic, cadmium, nickel, silicon, tin, and vanadium. These are present in smaller amounts.

All foods contain minerals, which are inorganic elements that are chemically more stable and less subject to losses when cooked than are the organic elements. Minerals have many functions in the body. They are absorbed in the intestine and transported into the blood and then to other body parts. Minerals all work together just like vitamins to keep the body in check! For example, the predominant acids in fruits are organic acids, which are metabolized fully by the body. Even acidic fruits such as lemons are base forming in the body. This is because an alkaline residue of sodium and potassium remains after metabolic breakdown of the organic acid. However, cranberries, spinach, rhubarb, chocolate, tea, and caffeine all contain acids that are not metabolized, and remain acidic. This is why cranberry juice is so often used to clear up urinary tract infections, because it remains acidic, as well as the others I mentioned.

Milk is both acid-forming and base-forming, since it contains phosphorus which is acid-forming and calcium which is base-forming, and the two neutralize each other. Minerals that are acid-forming are chloride, sulfur, and phosphorus. Calcium, magnesium, potassium, and sodium counterbalance the acid minerals because they are alkaline- or base-forming. There is an important communication that is going on in your body between all nutrients as they all work together to achieve a healthy equilibrium! All the nutrients I'm about to discuss all fit together and need each other to work!

A lot of people ask me what chelated vitamins and minerals are? Chelated (chē- lā- ted) means the binding of a mineral like iron to another substance for better absorption. For example, *amino acid chelate* means an amino acid (protein) which is extracted from yeast or vegetable protein and is attached to iron, chromium, or manganese.

FATIGUE: IRON

Iron is important for men and women, and the iron level in the body is maintained primarily by regulation of the amount absorbed in the intestine. If the body needs more, it will absorb the necessary amount. If you are a chronic dieter, taking an iron supplement is a wise choice to meet the RDA's requirement for 18 milligrams. If you decide to take an iron supplement, take it with vitamin C, because it is absorbed better in an acidic environment. It is the hydrochloric acid in the stomach that increases iron absorption, breaking it down from ferric iron to the ferrous iron form that the body can use.

It has been suggested that iron can interfere with vitamin E absorption, but only iron in the form of ferrous sulfate and phosphate interferes. Ferrous gluconate, peptonate, citrate, or fumarate do not interfere with vitamin E absorption.

Your red blood cells have a longevity of about four months. When no longer needed, a cell is removed from circulation and destroyed, usually in the spleen. Then the iron present is attached to a protein carrier and returned to the bone marrow to be used over again in synthesizing new red blood cells.

Iron is needed for the transport of oxygen to the cells and carbon dioxide away from the cells. If your cells don't get enough oxygen and carbon dioxide isn't carried away, it can cause fatigue, headaches, shortness of breath, weight loss, and hyperactivity, commonly referred to as iron deficiency anemia. Iron deficiency anemia is a condition that can be caused by too little iron in the body. Excessive iron can cause the same symptoms as anemia. This can cause confusion, which is why it is important get a blood test. Menstruating women have a greater need for iron and a greater risk for anemia.

Coffee, tea, eggs, alcohol, antacids, antibiotics like tetracycline, and too much fiber can all interfere with iron absorption. Iron from animal products is absorbed more readily than non-heme iron from plants. Some sources of iron are meats, liver, eggs, green leafy vegetables, legumes, raisins, dates, nuts, prunes, enriched and whole grain cereals, oysters, and clams.

I've have had many clients exhibit the symptoms I described, yet iron wasn't the problem. It could be a deficiency of B_{12}, which is needed to produce red blood cells. B_{12} deficiency is called *pernicious anemia*. Inadequate vitamin E and A can cause destruction of red blood cells. Folic acid and B_{12} are intertwined biochemically and are important to red blood cell production. Having enough protein is important also, because in your body iron combines with protein to form hemoglobin, the red substance in the blood that carries oxygen throughout the body, and B_6 is required for protein synthesis.

Hemoglobin is the oxygen-carrying pigment in the blood. Iron is also found in myoglobin, which carries oxygen from the blood to the enzymes in the muscle cell to produce energy for muscular activity. Many times getting enough iron is difficult even for the good eater, so it is important to eat well and take a iron supplement of 18 milligrams for one week out of the month unless you are anemic, in which case you need to see your doctor to determine how much iron you need. I suggest this because iron is stored in the body, and too much iron can cause the same symptoms as too little.

CALCIUM: KEEPING CALM

Did you know that there is more calcium in the body than any other mineral? The RDA for calcium is 1000 milligrams for adults and children four years and older.

The average American gets about 450 milligrams of calcium from food, which is not enough to meet RDA requirements, especially for a person who doesn't want to eat dairy products. A good amount of calcium is found in skim dairy products without the additional fat. To prevent bone and calcium loss as we get older, we need additional calcium, ranging from 1200 to 1500 milligrams daily, especially for women. This becomes a concern due to the lowering of estrogen levels after menopause; the extra calcium will help in the prevention of *osteoporosis* (brittle bones). People who are thin and small-boned are also at greater risk. Lower estrogen leads to bone loss because as estrogen decreases from the ovaries the secretion of hormones changes and draws out more calcium from the bones. It is estrogen that helps in calcium absorption.

The fat cells can also convert hormones released by the adrenal gland into estrogen. This is why, as fat is lost, estrogen production often decreases and may result in absence of the menstrual cycle. This occurs because estrogen is part of ovulation.

Calcium and phosphorus work together in a 2:1 ratio to maintain strong bones and teeth. Calcium is absorbed in the upper part of the small intestine, where it is more acidic. This is why it is good to take vitamin C with calcium to increase absorption. Calcium carbonate is a good supplemental form of calcium because the calcium makes up more of each molecule than lactate or gluconate forms of calcium.

Another good supplement to use is Calcium Night by Source Natural. Calcium works on the central nervous system to keep you calm, is involved in muscular contractions, and can help alleviate muscle cramping.

One abundant source of calcium is Swiss cheese, which is high in calcium (270 mg per ounce) and lower in sodium than other cheeses. Other sources are yogurt, milk, sunflower seeds, blackstrap molasses, sardines, tofu, and vegetables like broccoli and kale, as well as the supplement.

Calcium is lost when too much whole grain, which contains phytic acid, spinach and rhubarb, which contain oxalic acid, and tea, which contains tannic acid, are eaten. These acids all can prevent calcium and iron absorption. Don't go overboard with calcium, though. Too much can cause your blood levels of magnesium to decrease and zinc levels and blood coagulation to become imbalanced. If you have a history of kidney stones, you should consult your doctor before taking calcium supplements. Kidney stones are not only caused by calcium, but also by oxalic acid, which binds to calcium to form insoluble crystals (kidney stones) called calcium oxalate. Although kidney stones can be caused by the malfunctioning of the parathyroid gland, it is the parathyroid gland that triggers resorption of calcium from the bones to keep serum calcium levels normal, around 10 milligrams of calcium per 100 milliliters of serum. The thyroid hormone counterbalances the action of the parathyroid gland by removing excess calcium from the serum, preventing abnormally high levels of calcium.

POTASSIUM AND LOSING FAT

Everyone needs potassium. Your body contains about 300 grams. Your muscles use potassium, and without it you couldn't move. You need potassium to be able to think, because it is part of a process that converts glucose to energy that the brain cells can use. As you lose fat you are also losing potassium; you may start to feel fatigued and dark lines may form under your eyes. The purging of food causes loss of potassium and an imbalance in the potassium/sodium pump! The Recommended Daily Allowance is between 1525 and 4575 milligrams. Hyperkalemia is a condition involving too much potassium, which can cause damage to the heart, and even death. Check with your doctor to find out how much potassium you need. You can find potassium included in a complete vitamin and mineral supplement ranging from 4 milligrams to 99 milligrams.

You may need more potassium if you're eating too much sugar or protein, or if you continually use aspirin, cortisone, antibiotics, coffee, or diuretics. Potassium is needed for muscle contractions and peristaltic action, which is the muscles moving food through the digestive tract. If this doesn't function properly, constipation can result. The heart is also a muscle, and a potassium deficiency can cause a heart attack. Some foods that have potassium are bananas, cabbage, avocados, dates, prunes, apricots, raisins, potatoes, wheat germ, whole wheat, soybeans, legumes (nuts, seeds, beans), and fish.

MAGNESIUM: A PARTNER TO POTASSIUM

Yes, potassium and magnesium are partners and need to be and share in similar functions. Magnesium is important to the life of every cell, and it is a coenzyme needed for several biological processes. Magnesium is involved in the energy systems ATP (Adenosine Triphosphate) and Coenzyme A, which is needed for muscle energy, and like calcium it has a calming effect on the central nervous system. It helps with digestion, so you keep eliminating; too much can cause diarrhea. Both magnesium and potassium are needed for protein production, but too much can cause a loss of these nutrients. As you can see, more is not necessarily better! Your hormones, hair, skin, and nails need magnesium to be healthy and strong. Calcium works with magnesium in a 2:1 ratio, and folic acid and vitamins D, B_6, E, and C help both magnesium and potassium function.

The RDA for magnesium is 350 milligrams for ages 19 and older. In working with people who have poor food habits or are purging, hair loss, brittle nails, and digestive problems are some symptoms of magnesium deficiency. Start eating green leafy vegetables, grains, and legumes, like nuts, seeds, and beans. Some foods that bind magnesium, making it unavailable for use, are rhubarb, spinach, and chocolate, which contain oxalic acid, and grains that contain phytic acid. You can eat these foods; just don't eat too much. Use moderation with all food, or if you take a magnesium supplement, don't take megadoses. Always consult a doctor or other professional.

CHLORIDE AND DIGESTION

One of the most important roles chloride has is the production of hydrochloric acid in the stomach, so you can digest your foods and then absorb their nutrients. The RDA for chloride is 1400–4200 milligrams per day for adults, and the majority of chloride is found in the secretions of your digestive tract. Table salt is a source of chloride, as well as meats, milk, and eggs. Diarrhea and vomiting cause a severe loss of chloride, resulting in a dangerous imbalance in your electrolytes, and in constipation. If you can't break down your foods you can't absorb nutrients from them, and will begin to suffer from a number of nutritional deficiencies if the deficiency is not corrected. Too much chloride can upset the balance of acids and bases in body fluids.

CHROMIUM AND SUGAR

Sugar craving can sometimes be caused by low blood sugar levels. It is chromium that helps glucose move from the bloodstream into the cell. After you eat food, your body transforms the carbohydrates, protein, and fat into energy in the form of glucose. Chromium is an essential nutrient and is needed for maintaining normal glucose levels. Therefore, chromium helps to transform food into energy so you can feel alert. Both chromium and vitamin C are needed for your eyes to focus clearly. Chromium activates vitamin C. There is no RDA for chromium, but 50-200 micrograms is suggested by data from government studies.

Chromium is vital to GTF (glucose tolerance factor) production and is found in the center of GTF. There is no RDA for chromium or GTF, but the more sugar you eat, the more you need GTF to work with insulin. GTF is made of niacin, glutamic acid, glycine, cysteine, and of course, chromium. Foods that contain chromium are vegetables, fruits, whole grains, wheat germ, and brewers yeast, or nutritional yeast. GTF can be found in health food stores and will help reduce your sugar craving. Remember, you must also control your mind!

ZINC AND ITS MANY FUNCTIONS

Everyone needs zinc, and the RDA for zinc is 15 milligrams for a person 11 years and over. A zinc deficiency can cause fatigue, because it is zinc that transports carbon dioxide in the blood from the cells back to the lungs to get rid of it. Zinc is important for your ability to taste food and have a healthy appetite. Vitamin A couldn't be pulled out of storage from the liver without the help of zinc. Zinc is necessary to produce the protein needed to make DNA and RNA, as well as the sex hormones. Zinc is important to the functioning of insulin, and is found in the hemoglobin of red blood cells, protecting them from destruction.

The stomach needs zinc to produce hydrochloric acid. Zinc therefore helps other nutrients to be absorbed. Your teeth and gums need zinc, or your gums may bleed. Purging causes the loss of zinc and a wearing away of the enamel on teeth. Foods that contain zinc are eggs, liver, poultry, milk, fish, peas, soybeans, mushrooms, whole grains, nuts, and seeds.

VITAMIN A: EAT YOUR CARROTS

There is so much stress that comes from the polluted air we breathe (the ozone, heavy metals, carbon monoxide), and from food additives and much more, it's a wonder the body can withstand it all!

Vitamin A can help by protecting and strengthening your cellular membranes, which are needed to keep every tissue in your body healthy. Both vitamin A and E protect the gastrointestinal tract from ulcers and from the damage caused through purging, but it can only take so much abuse. Your body really knows how to take care of you until it is pushed too far. Vitamin A is important also to red blood cell production.

Vitamin A occurs in two forms: preformed vitamin A from the animal source, known as retinol, and proformed vitamin A from plants, known as carotene. Both retinol and carotene have a RDA of 5000 international units (IU) for adults and children four years and older. Preformed vitamin A (retinol) is found in eggs, liver, milk, and fish, whereas proformed vitamin A (carotene) is found in brightly pigmented yellow, orange, and dark green vegetables and fruits, such as carrots, spinach, squash, papaya, sweet potatoes, and peaches. It is beta carotene (available in supplement form) that is converted upon the body's demand by the mucosa of the small intestine to active vitamin A which the body can use. For every one molecule of beta carotene two molecules of vitamin A (retinol) are formed. Vitamin A is important in bone development and healthy skin, and it reduces the chances of infection.

GETTING YOUR B's

The B complex vitamins work together as a team. You should always take them together, and B_1, B_2, and

B_6 should be in a balance to work best. The B vitamins and vitamin C are known as *antistress vitamins*. All the B vitamins are important in the metabolism of carbohydrates, fats, and proteins, as well as for keeping a healthy intestinal flora. The B vitamins are found in rice, whole wheat, oatmeal, eggs, fish, cheese, yogurt, liver, peanuts, and most vegetables.

The RDA for vitamin B_1 (thiamin) is 1.5 milligrams for adults and children four years old and older. Vitamin B1 is destroyed by heat, sugar, and antacids.

The more sugar you eat, the higher your need for B_1. It is B_1 that promotes a healthy appetite, not overeating.

The vitamin B_6 (pyridoxine) is important to insulin utilization, hydrochloric acid production (needed for digestion), muscle contractions, and the breakdown of protein. This is why the higher your protein intake the higher your need for B_6. For example, B_6 is needed in order for tryptophan to be broken down to niacin (B vitamin) and to serotonin, a neurotransmitter in the brain that is important for appetite control and our ability to sleep. The RDA for B_6 is 2 milligrams for adults and children four years old and older.

THE ANTIANXIETY VITAMIN: INOSITOL

We all have stress, both psychological and physical. Eating problems are a combination of both, and create much anxiety. Inositol is an antianxiety vitamin that is part of the B complex family. It is found in both animal and plant tissue. In plant cells it is usually found as phytic acid, which is inositol hexophosphate. Your body manufactures inositol with the help of bacteria in the intestine. By now you should realize that you must have a healthy intestinal tract and good digestion in order for nutrients to be absorbed, and purging disrupts that healthy balance, which then disrupts other systems in your body.

Vitamin C and B$_6$ both help inositol function in reducing anxiety. Inositol is found in such foods as corn, wheat, oats, peas, barley, rice, beans, molasses, liver, and brewers or nutritional yeast. Inositol can also help you sleep. Inositol and vitamins B$_6$ and C can be purchased at any health food store.

THE POPULAR VITAMIN: C

The RDA for water-soluble vitamin C (ascorbic acid) is 60 milligrams for adults and children four years old and older. There are derivatives of ascorbic acid—sodium ascorbate and calcium ascorbate—which both function as a form of vitamin C, but don't contain the acid that can irritate the stomach. There is also a fat-soluble vitamin C called ascorbyl palmitate, which is sometimes used as a food preservative. I use the water-soluble vitamin C in crystal form and add it to fruit juices or sprinkle it on fruit salad to keep it from browning, maintaining freshness while increasing its nutritional value. It is important to get vitamin C from food sources. This is because the body cannot manufacture vitamin C. Vitamin C, like calcium, is needed for healthy bones, connective tissue, and iron absorption. It is connective tissue that cements the cells and tissues together. The principle component is the fibrous protein called collagen, which is found in skin, bones, and cartilage. Vitamin C is vital to collagen (fibrous protein) production.

Vitamin C serves an important function in the metabolism of proteins, changing tyrosine to thyroxine, which is important to thyroid production, and changing phenylalanine to adrenaline. Vitamin C also helps to keep the immune system healthy by increasing white blood cell production. I believe vitamin C can help in the prevention of colds. It is extremely useful to athletes, because they lose vitamin C through exercise.

Some good news is that vitamin C is abundant in most fruits and vegetables, like green peppers, strawberries, broccoli, tomatoes, oranges, and even potatoes.

It is vitamin C that changes iron from transferrin to ferritin, which is an iron and protein complex. Vitamin C helps tryptophan and amino acid convert to the neurotransmitter called serotonin, which helps you sleep! Tryptophan is very helpful for people with high anxiety and sleeping disorders. The thyroid gland and adrenal glands need vitamin C to produce hormones, such as thyroxine and adrenaline. The adrenal glands are referred to as your antistress glands, because they help you deal with stress, and a large amount of vitamin C is stored in the adrenals. Vitamin C in megadoses can cause gout and lower white blood cells' ability to kill bacteria. Don't think that more is necessarily better!

WHAT ARE BIOFLAVONOIDS?

Bioflavonoids are also called vitamin P, and they are closely related to vitamin C. The white inner skin of citrus fruits contains bioflavonoids. They belong to the flavonoid compound group. For example, rutin is part of the bioflavonoid family, and helps the healing of broken cells and tissues, and the lowering of high blood pressure. Citrin and quercetin are bioflavonoids that help with skin problems and relieve water retention in the tissue. Fruits such as oranges, plums, grapefruits, apricots, and cherries have bioflavonoids. You can also get a supplement that contains separate or individual bioflavonoids at your health food store.

VITAMIN D: LET THE SUNSHINE IN

The most common form of vitamin D is called cholecalciferol. Cholecalciferol is sometimes called D_3, and comes from animal sources, whereas, ergosterol, or D_2, is from plants. Vitamin D can be toxic in high amounts, so never exceed 1000 IU. The RDA for vitamin D is 400 IU for adults and children four years old and older. Some sources of vitamin D are eggs, cheese, yogurt, milk, tuna, and sunlight. Yes, sunlight (ultraviolet light) acts on the oils of the skin, synthesizing a form of vitamin D called 7-dehydrocholesterol. However, clothes and glass both block the ultraviolet rays, not allowing vitamin D to be produced.

Vitamin D is important for intestinal absorption of calcium. It also functions to prevent the formation of rickets in children and the adult form of rickets, osteomalacia. Healthy bone development and maintenance requires adequate amounts of vitamin D.

So, letting the sun shine through, you just might start feeling happier! As reported in the May 4, 1987 issue of *Newsweek*, Dr. Frederick Goodwin, of the National Institute of Mental Health, noted that in the fall and winter people suffer more from depression. This phenomenon is called seasonal affective disorder (SAD). He also noticed that people eat more carbohydrates from October through March, and these people need more sunshine in their lives! Dr. Goodwin suggests there is a hormone called melatonin, which is produced in the dark, and when people are depressed they tend to sleep more and therefore are exposed to even more darkness, possibly worsening their depressed state. He uses a "Sun Box" which mimics natural sunlight. So light up your life and get some vitamin D at the same time!

VITAMIN E: THE SEXY VITAMIN?

Several years ago I was working at a health food store, serving customers, when a man asked me where the vitamin E was because he wanted to be sexier! As I walked him to the vitamin E shelf, I told him vitamin E won't make you sexier, but it will make you healthier. He look distressed, and told me his girlfriend didn't think he was sexy enough, and he still bought a big bottle of vitamin E, and left, hoping I was wrong. A week later he returned with the vitamin E, and told me he decided to just get another girlfriend!

There is a rumor that vitamin E is an antisterility vitamin. This misunderstanding comes from the word for vitamin E—tocopherol—which comes from Greek, meaning "to bear children." Vitamin E can help vitamin A perform its function better in the body, and can keep your skin healthy and supple, but won't improve your sex life!

Vitamin E (tocopherol) has an RDA of 30 IU for adults and for children four years old and older. Vitamin E is fat-soluble and is stored in the fatty tissue, liver, heart muscles, testes, uterus, blood, and the pituitary and adrenal glands. It is an antioxidant, preventing oxidation of fats, while protecting vitamins A and C and selenium (a mineral) so they can perform their functions. Vitamin E helps to speed up the healing of burns, and supplies more oxygen to the body, increasing endurance, as well as protecting your lungs against air pollution. Leafy green vegetables, wheat germ, eggs, butter, liver, whole grain products, and vegetables all are good sources of vitamin E. Too much vitamin E, however, can be dangerous.

SOURCES AND IMPORTANCE OF SODIUM

Did you know that sodium is found not only in salt but in a number of other foods? Salt is made up of 60% sodium and 40% chloride. Sea salt it is no better than regular salt; it just costs more. Sea salt does not necessarily contain more minerals, because it has to be purified to meet government regulations.

The RDA for sodium is 1000–3000 milligrams daily. Even water, when softened, contains sodium. The sodium added to the hard water pushes out calcium and magnesium (which cause hardness), making water soft. The harder the water to begin with, the saltier the softened water will be. There are about 275 milligrams in two quarts of softened water.

There is nothing bad about sodium in and of itself; it is consuming too much that causes problems. Sodium is needed to maintain acid/base balance, and is even responsible for the transmission of nerve impulses and maintenance of osmotic pressure.

If you need to reduce your sodium intake, try a salt substitute like potassium chloride, which has the taste and texture of salt, but no sodium. You don't want to use ammonium chloride because it can irritate the stomach. Use salt substitutes in moderation. Exceeding a teaspoon a day could lead to hyperkalemia (high levels of potassium in the blood) and possible heart attack. Always consult your doctor before you switch to salt substitutes.

Some other sources of sodium are baking soda, baking powder, monosodium glutamate (MSG), and brine, which is table salt and water used in pickling, making corned beef, and canning and freezing foods. Most processed foods contain sodium in the form of disodium phosphate, sodium alginate, sodium benzoate, sodium propionate, or sodium sulfite. Can you see why it is so vital to read labels and become food wise? If you take care of your body, *it* will take care of *you!* Give your body a chance to work for you. It will be well worth your patience. You *deserve* to be healthy and happy!

13

Stop Putting Your Life On Hold

Every time you put your emotions on hold, *you also put your life on hold*. This is because you are never saying or doing what you really want or feel. By holding back and not expressing your true feelings, you begin to deprive yourself, emotionally and physically. You may find yourself turning to or away from food for comfort and control, focusing on a more superficial problem instead of on the real cause. Food can be used for emotional support, and fat for some people is an emotional insulator.

Saying what you feel means you take the risk of someone else not liking what you say, or of possibly even offending someone. The more you take the risk of saying what's on your mind, the better you'll feel and the closer you'll come to fulfilling your needs. How *are* you? Ask yourself this question and write a letter to yourself. This is a question we ask a lot of people each day, right after we say "Hi!" Only this time, really dig deep into this question—*Just how are you?* When Phil asked this question, he learned a lot more about himself, noticing he was feeling one way, but always acting another.

PHIL

Phil, at age 30, was an insurance man who came to see me because he was upset about gaining weight, and felt he was losing control. Phil told me he was a "Softie," and a real sensitive guy. He then referred to himself as a "sucker." Phil made sure that everyone around him was happy, even at the expense of his own happiness. He was not only afraid of offending others, but he was also seeking their acceptance. As I began to work with him, he discovered how expressing how he felt could be done without losing friendships, sometimes even strengthening them.

Step by step, Phil worked at self-expression; he was surprised to see how understanding his friends were. His fear of loss of control was not a fear of gaining weight, but actually a fear of losing his direction in life, by always doing for others and not for himself. He grew up in a large family and was used to doing things for everyone until he was exhausted. Pleasing others was a very loving and compassionate part of Phil, but he needed to become more self-concerned—*not* self-centered. The more *self-concerned* he became, the healthier he was, and he was giving other people a chance to give to him.

The more you deprive yourself of your own happiness, as Phil was doing, the more you dislike yourself and push even more to be helpful to others in hopes of feeling better. Then everyone around you thinks you're wonderful, except yourself! You put your life on hold while others fulfill their needs. Fulfilling your needs means you have a healthy concern for yourself—you are *self-concerned.* Learning to say "no" is essential to making the time you need—for *your* needs. It is okay to say "yes" to yourself and "no" to someone else.

LIVING IN THE FUTURE

Another way many of us put our lives on hold is by living in the future, while the here and now slowly dies, due to lack of attention and caring. Have you ever said to yourself, "Once I lose weight, then I'll be happy," or, "Once I have a relationship, or a car, or when the kids grow up, etc., *then* I'll be happy." Whenever I hear this comment from a client, I ask, "Why don't you deserve to be happy *now?*" "What are you depriving yourself or punishing yourself for?"

Don't wait to be happy! You *deserve* to be happy and fulfilled in the here and now. Depriving yourself only makes achieving your goals much more difficult. Ideally, you want to be happy in the present, while planning for the future.

Don't wait until next year, next week, or even tomorrow to improve your life. *Do it now!* Ask yourself "What can I do *now* to feel better about myself, that will result in positive change?" Putting things off leads to doubt and loss of not physical weight, but self-esteem.

If you feel your life is on hold, close your eyes and imagine that you have already accomplished your goal, and allow yourself to *feel* what it is like to have succeeded! Really try to *feel* the happiness, satisfaction, and peace of mind.

It is also easy for you to get hung up on old beliefs and attitudes about yourself, even if they are not true, and get stuck in a negative self-image. Overcoming your eating problem gives you a wonderful opportunity to get to know yourself, and believe in your potential, letting your strengths shine through.

No matter how beautiful you are on the outside, if you don't feel beautiful inside and like who you are, the mirror reflection will never be good enough, beautiful enough, or thin enough.

Put an end to fad dieting and self-deprivation. Be kind and compassionate to yourself! You're a special and unique person; start *caring* for yourself. It is time to start believing in your own potential!

YOU DESERVE TO BE HAPPY!
CHAPTER SIX: THINGS TO REMEMBER

* You are putting your *life* on hold when you put your *emotions* on hold.

* Ask yourself, "How am I?"

* Be happy *now*. You deserve to be happy. Say this to yourself as many times in a day as possible.

* Ask yourself, "What can I do now that make a positive change in my life?" Write it down!

* Close your eyes and imagine that you have already accomplished your goal. How does it feel? Feel the happiness, and satisfaction from all your work. Take time to really feel this wonderful peace of mind! Feel the excitement of success.

* Overcoming your eating problem gave you the wonderful opportunity to better understand yourself and use your potential to succeed. Many people go through life never getting to know themselves or learn the importance of caring for themselves.

Bibliography

Ald, Roy. *Jogging, Aerobics, and Diet.* New York: American Library Publishing Co., Inc., 1968.

American Heart Association. *The American Heart Association Cookbook.* New York: Ballantine Books, 1984.

Bass, Maryann, Kathy N. Kolasa, and L. Wakefield. *Community Nutrition and Individual Food Behavior.* Minneapolis, MN: Burgess Publishing Company, 1979.

Bland, Jefferey. *Year of Nutritional Medicine.* New Canaan, CT: Keats Publishing Inc., 1985.

Bloomfield, Molly M. *Chemistry and the Living Organism.* New York: John Wiley and Sons, Inc., 1980.

Buist, Robert. *Food Intolerance.* San Leandro, CA: Prism Press, 1984.

Butler, Charles M. *Neuropsychology: The Study of Brain and Behavior.* Belmont, CA: Brooks/Cole Publishing Company, 1968.

Cameron-Bandler, Leslie. *Solution.* San Rafael, CA: Published by Future Pace Inc., 1985.

Chaplin, J. P. *Dictionary of Psychology.* New York: Dell Publishing Co., Inc., 1968.

Crapo, Lawrence. *Hormones: The Messengers of Life.* Stanford, CA: Stanford Alumni Association, 1985.

Dignan, Mark, Marvin Levy, and Janet H. Shirreffs. *Essentials of Life and Health.* New York: Random House Publishing Inc., 1984.

FDA Consumer Vol. 18 No. 1. Rockville, MD: U.S. Department of Health and Human Services, HHS Publication No. FDA (83-1001), February, 1984.

Gates, June C. *Basic Foods.* New York: Holt, Rinehart, & Winston, 1981.

Holmberg, Rita. *Meal Management Today.* Belmont, CA: Wadsworth Publishing Company, 1983.

Lecos, Chris. *Tracking Trace Minerals.* Rockville, MD, Dept. of Health and Human Services, FDA Consumer HHS Publication No. FDA (83-2176) August, 1983.

Leibovitz, Brian. *Carnitine: The Vitamin B+ Phenomenon.* New York: Dell Publishing Co., Inc., 1984.

Mannerberg, Don, and June Roth. *Aerobic Nutrition.* New York: Berkley Books, 1983.

McClintic, Robert. *Physiology of the Human Body.* New York: John Wiley and Sons, Inc., 1975.

Mennler, Ruth L. *The Human Body in Health and Disease.* Philadelphia, PA: J. B. Lippincott, Company, 1970.

Mervyn, Leonard. *Thorsons Complete Guide to Vitamin and Minerals.* Rochester, VT: Thorsons Publishers, Inc., 1987.

Mindell, Earl R., and Richard A. Passwater. *Volume 2: Octacosanol, Carnitine, and Other Accessory Nutrients.* New Canaan, CT: Keats Publishing, Inc., 1982.

Mindell, Earl R. *Vitamin Bible.* New York: Warner Books, Inc., 1985.

Null, Gary. *The Egg Project.* New York: Four Walls Eight Windows, 1987.

Sahley, Billie J. *The Anxiety Epidemic.* San Antonio, TX: The Watercress Press, 1986.

Santillo, Humbart. *Food Enzymes.* Prescot Valley, AZ: Hohm Press, 1987.

Sloane, Ethel. *Biology of Women.* New York: John Wiley and Sons, Inc., 1980.

Wades, Carlson. *Amino Acids Book.* New Canaan, CT: Keats Publishing, Inc., 1985.

Williams, Melvin H. *Nutrition for Fitness and Sports.* Dubuque, IA: Wm. C. Brown Company, Publishers, 1983.

Winter, Griffith H. *Complete Guide to Vitamins, Minerals, and Supplements.* Tucson, AZ: Fisher Book Publishing, 1985.

Worthington-Roberts, Bonnie S. *Contemporary Developments in Nutrition.* St. Louis, MO: The C. V. Mosby Company, 1981.

Reflection of raindrops upon a face
Vision of a dream that's just been erased

Fantasy rainbow to each our own
Sharing together, we stand alone

Elegant equipage bought by the dollar
Beauty's only skin deep—within is the power

Portraying emotions essential for all
Silenced in solitude, with no one to call

Mystical Force allows to discover
Through standing alone, we do need each other

Loneliness and heartaches will soon be released
To someone who cares and faith will keep

Sprinkling laughter and joy to mankind
Hoping the search within he will find

Caring and sharing is all it takes
A part of your heart and a warm embrace

Cherishing moments of time spent together
Friendship treasured forever and ever

— Ilene Sue Haskin

New Outlook   Mind & Body

Listed below are tapes that can provide you with further insight on self-motivation, relaxation, and nutrition. Each tape is $9.95 plus shipping and handling.

_____ *Emotional Weight* ($12.95)

      Tapes ($9.95 each)
_____ Discover Your Potential
_____ Sweet Dreams (Relaxation for Children)
_____ Stress Busters
_____ All About Vitamins and Minerals

_$1.50_ shipping & handling

_____ Total

(Quantity discounts available.)

___ VISA   ___ check enclosed
___ Mastercard   ___ money order
___ American Express

Card #: _____ Expires _____
Signature: _____

Or Call 916-395-8010

New Outlook
6373 Riverside Boulevard
Sacramento, California
Box 114   95831

Please allow 4–6 weeks for delivery.

Listed below are tapes that can provide you with further insight on self-motivation, relaxation, and nutrition. Each tape is $9.95 plus shipping and handling. You can also order more copies of *Emotional Weight* using this order form or the **toll-free number** below.

_____ *Emotional Weight* ($12.95)

Tapes ($9.95 each)
_____ Discover Your Potential
_____ Sweet Dreams (Relaxation for Children)
_____ Stress Busters
_____ All About Vitamins and Minerals

_____ 4% tax for Michigan Residents only

 $1.50 shipping & handling

_____ Total

(Quantity discounts available.)

___   VISA   ___   check enclosed
___   Mastercard   ___   money order
___   American Express

Card #: _____   Expires _____
Signature: _____

Or CALL TOLL-FREE 1-800-533-1309.
VISA, Mastercard, and American Express accepted.

New Outlook
P.O. Box 15437
Ann Arbor, MI 48106-5437

Please allow 2 weeks for delivery.

√